Praise for *H*

Elizabeth Eddy will take you on a magic carpet ride of transformation. In these challenging times, Reiki's profound stress relief works for your mind, body, and emotions, to release your past traumas, relieve your present pain, and unlock your future.

– Jennifer McLean, creator and author of *Spontaneous Transformation Technique,* healer, speaker, and CEO of McLean MasterWorks

I appreciate Elizabeth Eddy's intention to demystify Reiki using easy to understand concepts along with ways to incorporate the many healing benefits into our busy lives. One more valuable and simple practice for us all to add to our self-care toolkit.

– Pam Culley-McCullough, Ed.D

Just a few pages into Dr. Eddy's new book, *How Reiki Works*, I could already feel my stress level de-escalate. I immediately thought of 4 or 5 friends and colleagues who would love to receive this book from me. We need to disrupt the stresses of this time, and reset our energy in healthy ways. We'd also enjoy learning about Reiki and practicing it together.

– The Rev. Julia McKeon, M.M., M.Div

I am so glad I read Elizabeth Eddy's book, *How Reiki Works*. Her scientific explanations helped me understand Reiki better and, after having tried it several times now, it has helped to relax and feel at peace with myself.

– Kim Han, M.A., MLIS

How Reiki Works truly enriches my Reiki bookshelf. Elizabeth Eddy creates new perspectives on healing, and life in general. Her well-researched scientific facts and profound thoughts inspired and refreshed me, though I have more than 20 years of experience as a Reiki teacher. This is absolutely not "yet another Reiki book" like all the others.

– Alice Gelma, Author and Reiki Master

Whether you are interested in learning Reiki or have been a Reiki practitioner for years, *How Reiki Works* is an amazing resource. Dr. Eddy takes the "woo" out of it and shows the essential elements of Reiki. Why should you learn Reiki? Check out this book and you will find out!

– Chellie Kammermeyer, LRMT

How Reiki Works is perfect for the waiting room at my holistic health center! A casual reader can easily find fascinating information in just a few pages, anywhere in the book! Every Reiki teacher I know will be delighted!

– Julia Jun, Reiki Master teacher and practitioner

After nearly six decades of emotional turmoil resulting from early abuse, a female coaching client now writes, ".... My emotional landscape has stabilized. After only six months of conversations with Ms. Eddy, I am now exuberant. I have been able to clear out of my house all the things that kept painful memories alive in my subconscious. I have given away things that were heavy in my heart, to people who can appreciate and enjoy them. I have rearranged furniture as well, so that now my home is a place of joy and inspiration."

– C.M

Elizabeth Eddy has been my Lifecoach for the past year. Her wealth of expertise and experience has guided me in many areas of my life. As a Reiki Master she adds Reiki to help me easily find clarity when I have decisions to make. Elizabeth is a 5-star coach.

– Velma Dunkin

ELIZABETH EDDY PhD

HOW

Reiki

WORKS

ENERGY HEALING FOR STRESS RELIEF, AND THE SCIENCE BEHIND IT

How Reiki Works

Copyright © 2020, Elizabeth Eddy

The views expressed by the author in reference to specific people in their book represent entirely their own individual opinions and are not in any way reflective of the views of Capucia, LLC. We assume no responsibility for errors, omissions, or contradictory interpretation of the subject matter herein.

Capucia, LLC does not warrant the performance, effectiveness, or applicability of any websites listed in or linked to this publication. The purchaser or reader of this publication assumes responsibility for the use of these materials and information. Capucia, LLC shall in no event be held liable to any party for any direct, indirect, punitive, special, incidental, or any other consequential damages arising directly or indirectly from any use of this material. Techniques and processes given in this book are not to be used in place of medical or other professional advice.

No part of this book may be reproduced or transmitted in any form, or by any means, electronic or mechanical, including photography, recording, or in any information storage or retrieval system without written permission from the author or publisher, except in the case of brief quotations embodied in articles and reviews.

The material in this book is provided for informational purposes only. It should not be used as a substitute for professional medical advice, diagnosis or treatment. It is your responsibility to research the accuracy, completely and usefulness of opinions, services and other information found in this book. The reader is responsible for their own actions. Some names have been changed to protect the privacy of some individuals.

Published by:
Capucia, LLC
211 Pauline Drive #513
York, PA 17402
www.capuciapublishing.com

ISBN: 978-1-945252-67-9
Library of Congress Control Number: 2019915033

Cover Design: Zizi Iryaspraha Subiyarta www.pagatana.com
Layout: Ranilo Cabo
Editor and Proofreader: Simon Whaley
Book Midwife: Carrie Jareed

Printed in the United States of America

Preface

Although I'll tell you quite a bit about myself in the course of this book, those snippets are told within formal contexts, while making a point. I want to begin informally. I want to tell you how exciting Reiki is to me.

This book was spawned principally from teaching Reiki. As I pass on what I have learned, I find myself asking questions I never asked before. The questions are formed in a mindset formed in childhood, a fascination with bugs and birds, animals and, really, the entire natural world. I need answers framed in the same language that describes the human digestive tract and the formation of snow crystals.

I have always loved detail. That orientation made it seem easy to me to analyze problems and discuss solutions. That mind took to logic and philosophy like a duck to water. So – to teach, I study further. I learn and write.

Another primary impetus has come from my volunteering to serve on the Reiki Team at a nearby hospital. I'll tell you more about this later in the book. What's most important to the formation of my message to you is my experience there. We team members give a ten-minute free session to anyone in the waiting room who wants it. The session is done in a chair, seated, dressed as they wait to see a doctor. The intent is simply to calm them, so they can be refreshed and clear-headed for their appointment. Many have driven for hours, or come in by plane the day before, because the clinic is specialized. The university teaching hospital associated with it is renowned and its doctors are world-class. This appointment is a Big Deal.

Only ten minutes of Reiki reduces the stress level of most people a great deal. The magnitude of beneficial change excites me every time I do a shift. From that, and other experiences in clinical work, I can see how much help Reiki can be to most people suffering with a chronic condition. I want people to receive Reiki daily, especially those suffering from a chronic condition. I am writing to encourage everyone under stress, including the seldom-noticed stress of long-term illness, to learn Reiki and to practice it on themselves.

In the following chapters I share with you discoveries I have made that answer my questions. One major discovery has been how the deep rest that Reiki provides can also be key to releasing emotional problems. You'll find information, and well-grounded speculation. I hope you'll find and share my hopes for all of you.

Contents

Introduction

Have you ever heard of Reiki?

I am writing with the intent to de-mystify Reiki. Reiki is not magical, mystical or a product of imagination. Reiki, as a practice, came from Japan out of personal experience and Eastern philosophy, but it is not limited to its origin.

Yes, the word is in Japanese. Pronounced *RayKee*, "Rei" means Divine or Universal and "Ki" means Life Force. *Universal* simply means that it is an energy found everywhere in the universe.

Reiki is energy: real and ordinary energy. It has been measured, as I'll describe in detail in Chapter 6. The energy is extra-low-frequency; its frequency range falls within the range of energy generated by the brain.

Reiki energy comes out of practitioners' hands. Practitioners commonly transmit Reiki by placing the palms of their hands on clients, or by holding their hands a few inches away from clients. Reiki can be transmitted over a distance, either short (you can give Reiki to your feet without bending over) or long (Reiki II practitioners can send Reiki across a room, across town, across the state, around the globe). Reiki can also be transmitted over a distance in time, forward or backward. These latter two characteristics can be explained in the language of quantum physics, but we won't go into that in this book.

Reiki is NOT massage. No manipulation is involved. Clients do not remove their clothes. It is not necessary to remove shoes either, but many people do that just for comfort.

Usually, clients receive Reiki while sitting in a chair, or lying down. Relaxation is a major component in the effects of Reiki, so we want to position the body comfortably.

Reiki began as a hands-on practice to achieve physical healing. The progenitor of Reiki as we know it, Mikao Usui, stubbed his big toe and then held onto it for a few minutes. When he took his hand away, there was no bruise, and no bleeding. His toe was fine. Usui immediately believed that he had found his destiny – to be a healer.

Usui's story will be told in more detail later, along with stories of people who have used Reiki for physical, mental and emotional healing in their lives.

You have STRESS?

The human body has amazing natural processes to deal with diseases and conditions, unless those processes are blocked by stress. Stress abuses our body and lays its defenses open so that we become vulnerable to disease. Stress is *dis*-ease. Dis-ease interrupts our natural tendency toward health. Stress lies at the root of many of our diseases and conditions.

Stress is DIS-EASE that Reiki Rest resolves

My focus here is not on healing tumors or measles or kidney stones, although many books on Reiki do just that. I am recommending Reiki to *most* people for stress reduction. We are living in chronic stress at an unprecedented level and, as a result, people are suffering all sorts of symptoms, as well as contracting diseases that the body might once have been able to ward off. Autoimmune conditions are also increasing in prevalence.

We already know many ways to reduce stress. But who has time to exercise? Who knows how to eat right? Don't most of us use a dysfunctional palliative remedy (like beer, or ice cream, or whatever) because it is handy and familiar? It might not work well, but at least it is entertaining, for a while.

I'm writing to familiarize you with something that could be new to you: Reiki. You have to choose to use it. It is not addictive. It has no dangerous side effects. It does not cause complications with any medication. What do you have to lose? It takes time to read this. It takes courage and time to try Reiki. But you'll lose stress. You probably carry more stress than you know, and most of us will have more tomorrow.

You may be already thinking, that if you had time to rest at all, regular rest would do enough. Not so. Reiki energy is *bringing you to rest*. Many people are actually incapable of relaxing. Reiki can override your compulsion to stay active – if you allow it to.

Having no time to rest can be a circumstance – many people find it's necessary to work as many hours as possible, in order to survive. But even if more work is necessary, so is the best quality rest with the best outcome available. Reiki is more efficient than simple downtime, because it restores the body in more ways than merely sitting down or enjoying entertainment does.

Chronic conditions?

My second most important center of attention – second in sequence, but not in importance – is everyone with a chronic condition. Although you may be dealing with illness or physical debility as best you can, with the help of modern medicine, adding Reiki to your treatment methods will improve life significantly for almost all of you. Chronic conditions create stresses that burden your condition by adding aches, pains, worries and complications of all sorts.

Reiki rest reduces stress quickly and safely. Reiki can reduce pain, tends to regulate blood pressure, and improves both digestion and elimination. You might say, Reiki resets one's biological defaults.

Whatever chronic condition you may have, it is easy and inexpensive to learn Reiki in comparison to what you are spending on medical interventions. When you have been attuned to Reiki, you can practice it on yourself, for convenient relief. After you have used Reiki for a while you may be able to reduce or even eliminate some medications.

Why is the title "How Reiki Works"?

How Reiki Works is a phrase with a double meaning. *Remainder* is one meaning of *rest*. Some people have unusual perceptual abilities. The rest of us – the remainder – most of us, in fact – do not have super-powers of perception. But almost all of *the rest of us* can practice Reiki. We don't have to have special abilities or esoteric knowledge. We can be everyday super heroes.

The second meaning of *rest* is physical relaxation. Rest is the principal perception of those who receive Reiki, and rest is a benefit of enormous, neglected, incalculable value. Reiki rest is deeper and more satisfying, as you'll read in Chapter 1.

Relief of stress in itself can be a major contributor to health. The body's natural systems for maintaining health can begin to function normally, when stress is reduced. The human body has amazing abilities to heal itself and maintain its health.

What to do?

I expect that if you are reading this book, you are open to trying new avenues for healing as well as for maintaining wellness. You may already know that your doctor knows very little or nothing about Reiki, and might be suspicious of it if you mention it. Chapter 6 is especially pertinent for assuring you and your medical providers that Reiki is helpful, safe and not in conflict with any treatment they advise. Notice that I am not claiming that Reiki is an alternative to medicine. In my view, Reiki is a *complement*. Whatever medicine does, Reiki *assists*. Sometimes Reiki is sufficient in itself, but those cases are unpredictable.

This book, unlike 90% of books on Reiki, does not explain how to *do* Reiki. Instead, I aim to show readers how using Reiki can enhance and simplify any traditional treatment they may undergo. I recommend that you find a practitioner, try a treatment, and then find a teacher (your practitioner may be a teacher, too). When you begin to practice Reiki on yourself, you'll easily have more Reiki in your life. It's a good idea to continue to receive professional treatments, but adding self-administered Reiki will increase the frequency of treatment you receive. More is better. In later chapters, I show how early practitioners discovered and implemented this principle. You'll find examples of results of Reiki throughout this book.

Finding a practitioner or teacher of Reiki is as easy as typing "Reiki near me" into your browser. Reiki is not learned in the usual sense. The ability to do Reiki is acquired through a process called *attunement* or *placement,* led by a Reiki Master. Once attuned, anyone can practice Reiki. (The process of attunement will be thoroughly discussed in Chapters 6 and 7.)

One point I want to emphasize at the outset is that Reiki can do what it does for you without your needing to know a diagnosis. Also, Reiki does not require that a practitioner be able to diagnose any client energetically.

It is also important to realize that the "us" includes people who are physically challenged in ways that cannot be altered, such as people who have suffered accidents and lost limbs, or people born with what we call disabilities. Reiki is thought of as a hands-on practice, but the use of hands is not necessary. A person with only one useable hand, or none at all, can ask Reiki to flow by directing the energy with his or her eyes, or even simply by intention. Hearing is not necessary to practice Reiki, nor is being able to walk.

What is necessary is *intent*. Intend Reiki to flow.

So - Who needs Reiki?

Almost everyone needs Reiki.

Emotional health is indispensable. *Coping* with life does not actually eliminate stress. Almost everyone suffers stress in some area of their lives, and many of us live in chronically stressful situations. Retirement does not necessarily decrease stress. Neither does changing a life partner. Neither does winning the lottery. Life has a way of pursuing us until we solve the problems we unconsciously create. (See Chapter 2 if this rings a bell to you.)

And, of course, physical health is always a need. Whatever means you choose to attain health or maintain it, Reiki can be an important and relatively inexpensive tool to achieve relief from the stress of dealing with your condition and concomitant pain. I especially want to impress you to use Reiki if you are dealing with long-term challenges:

○ chronic conditions such as MS, fibromyalgia, Parkinson's, diabetic neuropathy or Chronic Fatigue Syndrome,

○ PTSD,

○ advanced heart disease or lung disease,

○ stroke with incomplete recovery,

○ multiple conditions at the same time, especially those in which medications conflict with each other,

○ one or more conditions that have proved difficult to diagnose, while you continue to believe that somewhere out there lies an answer.

See Chapter 3 for examples and encouragement.

Want to help someone?

I wrote this book to encourage anyone who is a caregiver or relative of a sufferer. You can learn Reiki, and provide more than moral support to your loved one. If your patient also learns Reiki, the two of you together can provide even more relief, and faster.

Those who want to help include nurses and physicians who have a passion for healing, yet are also always seeking precision regarding causes and effects. They have high regard for certainty and observable facts. There is a chapter especially for medical professionals: Chapter 6 - Reiki for Geeks.

I want to invite all nurses (you probably know about Reiki already) and physicians to learn Reiki and discover how it can benefit your patients, as well as yourself. I anticipate that newbies to Reiki will discover enhanced wellness and happiness for themselves and their patients, and therefore be able to offer a heartfelt recommendation to use Reiki.

Reiki can benefit the practice of nursing in subtle ways you might not think of. A nurse friend of mine, who uses Reiki in her work, told me, "When

I'm inserting an I.V., I gently hold the patient's arm and ask Reiki to flow. The I.V. inserts flawlessly." I'm sure her patients appreciate her service.

What do you want to read next? – TWO MORE POINTS

Please enjoy reading outside the box. When you go for Reiki, you are choosing to live outside the box of *medicine* as we know it. When you read, please enjoy your freedom. After all, Reiki is for REST. Read the parts that appeal to you, in the order that appeals to you. When you are satisfied, just go get attuned – and use Reiki.

If you have purchased this copy on Amazon.com, please submit a review of it there. Your review assists other people's purchase experience.

Chapter 1

STRESS? Reiki is the answer

"If you can keep your head when all about you are losing theirs, and blaming it on you ..."
(Rudyard Kipling, poem, "If.")

The biggest complicating factor for human health is the human mind. Human mental processes create chemicals and energies that interfere with the otherwise neat biochemistry of health. In other words: as we describe mind's action scientifically, every thought is a *real thing*. Each thought is, or corresponds to, a pattern of energy or a sequence of chemical changes in the body.

For instance, some thoughts are angry or fearful, and initiate adrenal action. Stressors, whether three-dimensional or beliefs, are agents that call on biological resources, such as the adrenal glands. Adrenaline, cortisol and a host of other chemicals are manufactured by the body and released into it in reactions designed to counteract stressors.

The eventual result of over-using certain adrenal-activating patterns of thought can be disease instead of natural health. On the other hand, reducing stress can increase the body's efficiency in processing the medications we use. Sometimes, fear delays us in going for treatment.

A friend of mine told me about her niece, daughter of one of her brothers:

"More than twenty years ago, when the family was living in Australia, my niece was born. When she began to learn to walk, her movements seemed awkward, and her parents asked the child's doctor about this behavior. Tests were done, and the diagnosis was juvenile arthritis.

Pain patches were prescribed, one each month, as well as medication. She seemed to develop anxiety about her monthly medical exam, so the family decided to assist. There were other brothers in the family, including twins. In that society and at that time, twins were considered to have the ability to heal. The twins cultivated that reputation by being attuned to Reiki by a woman who was the first in Australia to teach Reiki. The twins and the child's father together laid hands on the infant before each monthly appointment and change of patch. The twins were using Reiki, while the dad used loving concern. The anxiety symptom disappeared.

When the child grew into her teen years, the condition diminished in severity. Now she is a grown woman with no symptoms at all."

How much did Reiki do to heal the child's juvenile arthritis? We don't have enough information to answer that question, but it does appear that Reiki eased the child into her treatment routine.

There is another question I want to ask, and its answer is obvious. How many people lack STRESS in life? Not very many. We all seem to be multitasking. Even though a certain level and type of stress seems beneficial, built into us biologically, an enormous number of us live with dysfunctional levels of stress.

Reiki is simple. Reiki is easy. Anyone can practice Reiki. Anyone can use Reiki. Reiki induces relaxation for most people (this will be thoroughly discussed in Chapter 2). Ten minutes a day does wonders. You could hit the snooze button, lay your hands on your chest and allow Reiki to start your day. Too simple? Do you need a physical catastrophe to get going?

Stumbling blocks along my way

In fact, I did. I was attuned to first level Reiki in 1998, and second level twice in the early 2000s. I went for Master level in 2007. All that time, I thought Reiki was only for people who had physical problems. I knew that Reiki could be helpful to people with physical problems but I did not practice it on myself because I thought I was too healthy.

In 2009, I was surprised to be diagnosed with a genetic heart condition referred to by its acronym HCM[1].

Deterioration was so gradual that I didn't really take the diagnosis seriously. However, symptoms became challenging enough to take meds, and I was ready to choose open-heart surgery in 2015. It was scheduled for the day after Labor Day weekend.

Planning for surgery, I knew I wanted Reiki. I typed *Reiki at (the university teaching hospital near me)* into my browser and it returned the name of a Reiki professional, a woman who served at that hospital as a private contractor. I asked her for Reiki a couple of days before surgery, and for Distant Reiki in the recovery room. (Allowing a Reiki practitioner to be in the operating room physically is still unusual in 2019, and was not the practice at the hospital where I was being treated.)

---

1   HCM is the acronym for Hypertrophic Cardiomyopathy. The heart wall inside the left ventricle grows at an unpredictable rate and for no known reason. It is believed to be a genetic anomaly. This growth adds tissue to the inside wall of the ventricle. The excess tissue obstructs the flow of blood. Less blood flowing through one of the four chambers disrupts the heart rhythm and eventually displaces the aortic exit valve because pressure inside the heart increases. The condition is diagnosed by echocardiogram, which is not yet a routine test. (As a result, high school boys who have HCM can die suddenly on the football field.)

The days and months of recovery after surgery were really demanding, but I forgot Reiki again. I returned to my habits of *putting up with* and *waiting to see*, instead of adding Reiki to my physical therapy and ongoing medical treatment. I accepted slow progress.

By March 2016 I felt well enough to take a second Reiki Master class. I was already a Reiki Master. I had taken the ICRT (International Center for Reiki Training) Master class from William Lee Rand in April, 2007. But that was in his first system. His new system, called Holy Fire® Reiki (Holy Fire and Karuna Reiki are registered service marks of William Lee Rand), had been advertised for two years already in Reiki News Magazine. This Masters was not the usual thing, in my mind. The name of the system rang bells for me. "Want that!" I had said to myself emphatically.

The bell I heard said, "God is at work here." That did not mean God had not been at work in all my prior Reiki experiences. It meant, "Pay attention, this is important, don't miss this." (In traditional Judeo-Christian language, "Holy" refers to God, and "Fire" can symbolize "God at work".)

Holy Fire Reiki was received by William Lee Rand, creator of ICRT *(www.reiki.org)*. Rand wrote, "Holy Fire Reiki is a new form of Reiki that was introduced in January, 2014 by the ICRT. It is both powerful and gentle and provides purification, healing, empowerment and guidance." (See article "What is Holy Fire Reiki" at *https://www.reiki.org/ HF3.html*. You'll find more about William Lee Rand in Chapter 9.)

William Lee Rand and Colleen Benelli team-taught the Master class I took. Rand had had open-heart surgery on the same day as I had in 2015. But he was already vigorous. He challenged us all to long and strenuous hikes each afternoon in the vicinity of our class site in Hana, Maui. I sat on the beach instead, still dizzy and in pain. He had used Reiki on himself, and had been a center of concern for hundreds of people who sent Reiki daily. I was miffed, to say the least, at his energy, strength and stamina, but correct in my evaluation of my markedly decreased abilities at the time. Sitting on the beach was right for me then.

The Holy Fire II Master class was exhilarating; but despite the clear example of my teacher's amazing recovery, I continued my own by allowing nature to take its course, along with a few over the counter medications. After a summer of slow improvement, I fainted, fell, and hit my head. Then I struggled for months with post-concussion syndrome.

Despite the physical setback, the Masters' class had ignited me with fresh passion for Reiki, deeper and broader than I had experienced before. Practicing Reiki became more than a nice idea – it became an internal organic urge. I applied to join the Reiki team at the university teaching hospital where I'd had my surgery. I wasn't sure that I was sufficiently clear of dizziness to stand for a couple of hours at a time, but I pressed onward.

I begin to grasp the practical value of stress reduction

We in the Reiki team give free ten-minute sessions in a specialized clinic outpatient waiting room. We are not trying to heal anybody. We are simply offering supportive care – to anybody in our area waiting room, caregivers and family members included. We offer stress reduction. Often, headaches melt away and other pains subside noticeably. I hear recipients report deep relaxation, increased mental calm and clarity, and indefinable wellbeing and confidence.

Comments of appreciative patients and caregivers began to add up. I finally *got it*. Reiki, at the very least, induces a profound level of relaxation that releases the tensions we find or create, and then maintain unconsciously, by our daily worries, and fears, and *I don't knows*, and *I can'ts*. Ten minutes of Reiki clears enough stress and blocks to be able to face a challenging situation and a challenging medical appointment with mental clarity, ask appropriate questions, and plan for action. Ten minutes make a tough day doable.

Meanwhile, each session provides ten minutes of bliss for the practitioner – that deserves another chapter (Chapter 5).

I was hooked. Day after day, these experiences added up. I began to want to create studies of our results. In that situation, studying patients and caregivers was not possible, so I looked for scientific explanations – and I found some basic pertinent facts, starting with a prior interest of mine: meditation.

Reiki is meditation for your body

Are you one of the people who say you can't meditate because you can't get off the merry-go-round of thoughts in your head? Use Reiki to achieve similar results.

Scientific instruments became capable of measuring Reiki and Healing Touch energy during the 1990s. Reiki frequencies were found to range from 0.3 Hertz to 30 Hertz. The energy constantly pulses within that range. (You'll find a technical discussion in Chapter 6.) Hertz is the term used to refer to the frequency of a vibration. It is common terminology to refer to any range of frequencies as a bandwidth.

Frequencies coming from hands are the same as frequencies coming from the brain. The devices used to measure Reiki are different from devices that measure brainwaves, but the energy frequencies overlap. (This will be discussed in detail in Chapter 6.)

The slowest brainwave range is called Delta, 0 - 4 Hz. That range is associated with the deepest levels of relaxation, meditation, and restorative sleep. The Delta range is also involved with some unconscious functions such as regulating heartbeat. (Patients with chronic conditions have told me that their blood pressure tends to normalize during Reiki.)

The next range is the Theta range, 4 - 8 Hz. This range is associated with creativity, emotional connection, intuition, meditation and relaxation.

The Alpha range is 8 -12 Hz. When there is sufficient Alpha activity, we can calm down. When we become stressed, there is a common phenomenon called *Alpha Blocking* during which excessive Beta brainwaves seem to block production of Alpha brainwaves. The Alpha brain state at its optimal level is the condition of the brain at rest. There are quietly flowing thoughts, some meditative states and relaxation. The Alpha state is the *Power of Now*.

You can see that almost one-third of the Reiki bandwidth is the same bandwidth as found in meditation and deep sleep. It is no wonder then that Reiki is so often experienced as restful.

Although meditation is ordinarily spoken of as quieting the mind, the body also relaxes during meditation. The change works both ways – relaxing the body can relax the mind, as well as vice versa - because mind and body are not separate. During a Reiki session, both body and mind receive benefits similar to those of meditation. Besides relaxation, an important benefit is that during Reiki rest, when the mind relaxes, normal physical processes can occur with less interference from thoughts. In other words, Reiki allows the body to reset to normal healthy default systems.

The remainder of the Reiki bandwidth fits into the Beta brain wave range. For Reiki, that is 12 Hz to 30 Hz, while for the brain the Beta state is somewhat wider, 12 Hz to 38-40 Hz. Beta brain waves dominate our consciousness when attention is engaged by mental tasks and the outside world. The Reiki bandwidth does not range into the higher Beta levels that are associated with excitement. To me, this is consistent with the observation that Reiki brings clarity and order to our normal mind.

Meditation releases us into peace and freedom

Meditation has, for eons, been known to release the mind from bondage to attachments. We might suppose that the freedom we seek is simply freedom from dysfunctional patterns of emotion, but bondage also occurs in our thoughts.

The mind normally constructs relationships between ideas, and works with any structure until it breaks down in experience. For instance, if we grew up in a culture in which every person had brown eyes, we might assume that human eyes are always brown. We might say – too emphatically, but in honest mistake - "Human eyes MUST be brown." This normal thought process is how we arrive at racial profiling, for instance, or any other prejudice.

Reiki rest can release attachments that are dysfunctional. Then, our body tends to snap back to its original defaults.

Easier said than done! Or – always that easy – but we humans create mental and emotional complications for ourselves daily. Some complications are beliefs that were created in early childhood and became unconscious rulers of our emotions and behavior. As we grow up, unraveling those complications can become very important for us to be able to achieve our hopes and dreams. Unraveling can take time and intention, and Reiki can be amazingly helpful in the process.

The fact that one third of the Reiki energy bandwidth is the same bandwidth as meditation is key, I believe, to understanding how Reiki can be so helpful when we decide to release ourselves from dysfunctional beliefs, emotions and behavior patterns.

We usually think of relaxation as a function of our muscles. But the relaxation effect of meditation is a change in our mind that we monitor by changes in our thoughts. Commonly, people who meditate become calmer, and hold their opinions differently. Ideas in a meditator's mind link to each other less strictly, more fluidly. A meditator can examine his or her views more detached from emotional bias than other people. A meditator can easily adapt mentally to new data, and is alert to new possibilities of relationship. Using Reiki to meditate the body facilitates beneficial changes in our ideas.

Chapter 2 looks more deeply into how Reiki releases mental tensions that cause stress, and Chapter 3 examines how Reiki rest benefits people suffering chronic physical stress.

Chapter 2

Rest does more than we know

LIFE is a chronic condition

L ife is pesky. Problems keep showing up. How can we solve them? By creative, out-of-the box thinking. Does that come automatically? For a few, maybe. Is there a way to turn on that capability? Yes, there is: use Reiki.

What we want of life is chronic success. Better health, more strength, lasting happiness. Reiki is a simple and cost-effective way to attain better health.

Better health gives us more energy. Positive energy moves us toward accomplishing our dreams.

Stress is a killer

You know that already. Articles on that are too numerous to mention. Stress lies behind most major diseases, and unavoidably accompanies chronic conditions. We increase our level of stress by taking pride in our ability to multi-task. Hero stories are made of men and women who worked 20 hours a day all their lives. Is that heroism really sustainable? When you have a choice, don't you want heroism that succeeds in balancing work with satisfying family life as well as recreation and a modicum of self-care? Left to our natural devices, most of us would vote to prolong health as well as life.

The most natural stress-reliever is Reiki – reliable, and safe – no medication conflicts. Ten minutes or less pulls you out of unbelievable snarls. How long does it take for an over the counter medication to kick in? Really, as soon as we pop a pill, our mind settles down, *back to work as usual*, and we don't actually notice when we start to feel better. Are you satisfied with that technique? Can you use your drug-store meds till Kingdom Come with no side effects?

When you are too pressed for time, quick relief is your goal. Mine, too. That's why I give myself Reiki – briefly, but as often as I need to step away from stress. I choose to use Reiki to relieve stress as it comes, to avoid the build-up that inevitably saps our health and strength.

By the way, I want to make an important point here. I just used the word *give* to express my directing Reiki toward something, a person or object, or myself. But I'm about to encourage everyone to be attuned, and *give* Reiki to yourself, so I want to warn you to use the word *give* carefully. The word resulted in a hang-up I had for years, of failing to give myself Reiki when it could have been helpful. I suspect you might be affected the way I was. It doesn't make sense to *give* energy of your own to yourself. And when you feel low on energy, you certainly would never think of further depleting yourself. Truth be told, we'd rather *receive* care than give it to ourselves.

If that weren't hang-up enough, there is another real consideration: I really do not create Reiki. Reiki is a universal energy. I invite, I request, I allow. This does not mean that I imagine a sentient universal being – although there could be one. What I do is marshal my own energy. That is easy to do – I invite, I request, I allow. My energy simply *opens*. You may be able to feel this happening. Reiki energy responds to your request - just as metal filings respond to magnetism.

This change in language is important. When you are sick, or when you are tired, you feel you have nothing to *give*. So it might not easily occur to you to use Reiki on yourself. Instead, know that the only energy of your own that you use is to *invite Reiki*, or *allow Reiki*, or *ask Reiki*. Reiki will begin to flow, and Reiki will do what it does without instruction.

Returning to my prior point, the use of Reiki to relieve pain: many times, we are able to not only relieve our immediate pain but also gain value from awareness of the situation in which pain occurs. When we can observe ourselves, detached from our self-judgments, we can begin to learn about our personal behavior patterns.

A great deal of stress is virtually self-inflicted. That is, much stress results from beliefs we once formed innocently, to save our hide at the time. We create behavior patterns around beliefs we form in childhood. As time goes by and we learn more about ourselves and the world around us, our early beliefs often become dysfunctional. Until we take the time to look carefully at our patterns, we continue to repeat the stresses of unsolved inner conflicts. We can learn to identify these, and choose to change them.

The remainder of this chapter takes a deep dive into the process of releasing old inner conflicts. You'll see how easy Reiki rest makes these shifts.

Moving off the emotional pain-point

Reiki helps us in mind and in emotions, to sort through conflicting data or conflicting emotions, to arrive at a new plateau of understanding or a new resolution of emotional conflict. Reiki is a bandwidth, an organized energy that our mental confusions and physical tensions entrain to.

ENTRAINMENT is a name for a process that will be explained in detail in Chapter 6. In brief, the word refers to the fact that some stronger vibrations tend to dominate weaker vibrations. It's like the way a teenager can merge into a group of others and take on their prominent behaviors.

In an episode of the *Big Bang Theory*, Sheldon demonstrates how hard it is to get to an answer if one focuses only on the problem. Breaking away from a problem is necessary to release the mind from the patterns of thinking that are not working. Then we can allow a new pattern, an answer, to spring into place. Albert Einstein expressed this phenomenon by the assertion, "We can't solve problems by using the same kind of thinking we used when we created them." Even Einstein slept on it.

When you learn Reiki and use it on yourself, your ability to reach a state of calm is the first step you can take in a mental or emotional quandary. The result of Reiki rest is emotional stability. That clears your mind, making it easier to think. When you can think through your problem or emotionally trying situation, you usually find a solution easily. I use Distant Reiki often when coaching clients. In the midst of even a difficult emotion, such as anger, or jealousy, or rage, I direct Distant Reiki to my client over the phone. This quickly brings the client to the point of emotional stability or mental clarity needed to find a solution. After attunement, you can allow Reiki to flow to you when you find yourself in emotionally difficult situations.

Most people have developed ways to feel better that are really inadequate – we may scream (at other people), or use physical pacifiers, such as alcohol or drugs or food or cigarettes. You already know how the use of substances can often lead to abuse, and you may have despaired of finding better solutions. You could turn to Reiki. You could learn Reiki, and use it on yourself.

Some ways to feel better are verbal instead of substance. You've heard sayings that cool your emotions like, "This too shall pass." That is actually a statement of belief. When this sort of saying becomes automatic, psychologists call it a *coping mechanism*. We create beliefs that help us reduce stress in our life.

Have you noticed that we use these alternatives when our feelings are so strong that our rationality is compromised? Do we really want to live with compromised rationality?

The "I'm Fine" Coping Mechanism

How many times have you said, "I'm fine!" when you consciously knew you weren't? That asked, how many times do you think you could have said, "I'm fine!" when you were simply *not conscious* of an underlying layer of tension?

It can be useful to ignore tension. Certainly, our mind selects a range of content to deal with at any moment, and personal tension may be the least important of all data on our plate. But it flies in the face of our overall health and personal safety when we develop such a tolerance for stress that we say, "I'm fine," when we do not even sense we are not "fine." Our body, instead of our mind, registers stress. Stress shows up clinically as higher blood pressure, lower resistance to disease, and sometimes as autoimmune conditions. We could feel better than we do, even when we *think* we are fine. Reiki helps us feel better than "fine."

The Blaming Way to cope: "It's All in Your Head"

I remember as a child reading magazines for adults. At the time (1951 - I was 8), I noticed many articles discussing "nervous breakdown". It seemed to me to be a popular condition at that time. My mother tried it out then, for very good reasons.

That started me on a quest, looking at ailments and wondering what cause they might have in emotions. At that time, the prevailing attitude seemed to me to be blame. No matter what physical ailment showed up, there would be preceding emotions to blame it on. It seemed there was general consensus that emotions were often the root cause of illness.

It seemed to me that illness resulted in being blamed. ("Look what you did! Now I have to clean up after you!") The solution that I tried at the time was, "not to feel". I was coping. I didn't want to be sick, and I thought feelings were at fault. I had experienced hospitalization when I was three and again at six, and still remember loneliness and fear. I concluded that hospitals were not happy places to be, so I didn't want to go there again. But my attempts at coping – ignoring queasy feelings and odd pains, and cleaning up after myself when I was sick – was dysfunctional. It left me in a puddle of self-blame. Every pain and queasy feeling became a chance to blame myself for having those feelings – "I must have thought a 'wrong thought' or else I would feel fine." Blame was a tough habit to break.

I can't trace the process that broke the habit because I became so deeply involved in self-healing. As mentioned earlier, I experienced Usui/Holy Fire II Reiki Master training in March, 2016. I was still convalescing from open heart surgery, and physical healing continued throughout that year. But more than the physical, I needed emotional healing and renovation of some dysfunctional beliefs.

Reiki energy is present in every person and is activated by attunement (called "ignition" in

Holy Fire). In a period about six months after a Master's initiation, Reiki usually works to reframe one's internal emotional structure and life. After that period, I was able to work on myself in a whole new and amazingly effective way. I discovered the work of Jennifer McLean. (*Spontaneous Transformation Technique*, Jennifer McLean, ISBN -13: 9780988585522.) Check out her website at www.mcleanmasterworks.com. She does remarkable energy work, both by "dusting and cleaning", and by adding helpful energetic structures. She has the unusual ability to create attunements for specific purposes that tailor themselves to individual needs. She uses the term "attunements" because she was attuned to Reiki while developing her healing abilities.

Working with her created the first real emotional changes I had ever experienced. Many old bad habits broke. Many of my beliefs changed too, in beneficial ways. Beliefs I had struggled with for years clarified and simplified. Along my way through life, I had created beliefs for myself that had become so out-of-date with life as I grew, that they cried out for change. I had picked up dysfunctional beliefs from other people, too.

When I learned that one third of the Reiki energy is the same frequency band as meditation, I realized that Reiki in me had greased the wheels of my transformation process. Ultimately, I also understood how Reiki works with our emotions, and I began to use both McLean's technique and Reiki within my practice of Life Coaching.

One day a woman in the specialized outpatient clinic waiting room asked me to tell her about Reiki. She wanted to know because her daughter had been attuned to Reiki recently. What had her daughter gotten into? I attempted a short answer but the woman suddenly interrupted with an exclamation of happy surprise. "My daughter's personality changed completely!" she said. "How could that happen?"

I suddenly realized that what I had learned from Ms. McLean, together with my experience of Reiki, could explain a spontaneous positive character change. **Reiki fosters spontaneous healing of emotions because it induces very deep rest.**

Reiki rest is much deeper and more complete than normal rest because Reiki affects the brain as well as muscles. Working with Reiki, Jennifer McLean and her system, I began to be able to find and release many early traumas that had resulted in my ineffective coping mechanisms. Very deep Reiki rest enabled me to release my troublesome beliefs easily. My life transformed. I was amazed and delighted. It was an immense relief to me, to be able to reduce the unhelpful emotional chatter that kept me trapped in emotional reactivity, instead of being able to find rational solutions to problems as they arose.

There is a downside to my new life: I am now more grieved and appalled than ever by the fruitless furor so common in politics around the world today. Peace and prosperity could come so easily.

How? The Process, beginning at A

Emotions are energies in the body. Emotions can be triggered by thoughts. Thoughts are real. Thoughts are real *things* because they are real energy systems in our mind and body. Emotions, thoughts and beliefs are all energies.

We can think thoughts and beliefs that depress our immune system. This can occur when thoughts contradict each other.

Contradictory thoughts can niggle inside us unconsciously for years. We feel each contradiction as a tension. For example, you might have often heard as a child, "Don't speak to strangers!" Then as an adult, when in a room with a lot of strangers, you feel uncomfortable, and may habitually not speak a friendly greeting, without knowing why. As adults, we may interpret our tension as confusion, or blame ourselves for our withdrawn nature. We may expend energy to try to resolve our behavior, but not succeed because we don't see its real root.

Our immune system can also be compromised when we use a coping mechanism to avoid feelings. In that case the feelings are simply being repressed, and continue to plague us unconsciously. When the energy overload increases, we can become vulnerable to toxins. We say we are stressed.

Reiki is a tool we can use to help us simplify our belief systems. We can do this deliberately, or simply allow it to happen spontaneously. If we have a problem area in life or language, we can deliberately intend to clarify it, and look for situations that assist us in our endeavor. Reiki assists us in releasing the elements in our thoughts that cause our inconsistency.

For people who live without Reiki active in their life, dysfunctional habits often persist. For people who use Reiki, the action of Reiki inside the practitioner has a way of constantly improving mental as well as physical functionalities. The practice of Reiki clarifies thoughts and softens our attachment to beliefs that do not serve us personally.

We are accustomed to solving problems by using language. So-called talk-therapy is used to clarify ideas and feelings that we have held tightly. In talk-therapy we find new verbal structures that can free us from unnecessary tensions and confusions.

Our problems are not simply ideas perched on wires in our brain. Our problems are also chemical changes amid biological structures. The problems held in our tissues do not necessarily dissolve when we are not consciously focused on them.

As they say in yoga, "Issues are in the tissues." For example, we say we have a *stiff neck* when we have not yielded to a solution that lies in front of our nose. Or we say we have *a pain in the rear.*

We can seem to forget the origins of some of our issues, but memories of our struggles are actually stored, as much in body tissue as in our brain. The emotional source of the sore back may sink into the subconscious, and it may require effort to bring the struggle back into consciousness. But Reiki rest can loosen the bindings that keep some memories buried, and Reiki rest can soften the emotional charge that keeps us upset.

Clearly, the accusation "that's all in your head," is not accurate.

And, by the way, storage sites for memories in the body can be surprising. You might think of the liver, for instance, since the liver rids our body of toxins. Recently, however, I heard from a woman who had serious frightening experiences of sexual abuse as a young child. When she was able to release her attachment to fear aroused by those memories, her thumbs, which had been backward turning (as many people's are) released, and straightened into the more usual palm-turning configuration.

All tensions exist as energy that could be used for better living. The tensions that have been held since early childhood are seldom in our awareness. Those old unconscious tensions rob our energy field as much as conscious tensions do. We hold more tension than we realize, which is why people who think they are "fine" can feel really wonderful after receiving Reiki rest.

The Essential Release

When we deal with emotional issues and with stress in our life, we are accustomed to feel issues and stress as tensions held in the body. We tend to notice changes in our tension as a physical release. When releasing stress, you may feel tiny jerks or quivers from time to time, or sigh, or tears may leak out of your eyes. From the practitioner's point of view, these are just a few of many possible manifestations of release of tension.

When working with emotional issues, we sometimes relieve tensions by working with words. It can be helpful simply to *get clear* on meanings of words (like *love*) or talk through worrisome possibilities until a path emerges toward a hoped-for outcome. Reiki assists such release by providing deep rest, even during conversation. Tensions we are holding unconsciously can be released without conscious understanding of *what went*. We feel better when the session is done. Because our mind has clarified, solutions or decisions come more easily. It is not unusual to discuss problems with a Reiki practitioner before a session, and after the session leave with renewed energy, capable of handling your situation with a fresh perspective.

Release often occurs in context of the particular emotional goal being sought. You, as client, may intend to release yourself from obsessive grief, or from a dysfunctional behavior pattern, such as eating or drinking alcohol to find relief from stress. Some unconscious tensions can be released in the process of intentional conscious releases. Sometimes however, you may have a need to become conscious of a certain tension you have been holding, and uncovering the unconscious belief may take a bit of digging.

Remember the wife and mother I mentioned only a few pages ago? You may recall our conversation in the specialized clinic waiting room about Reiki and the positive effects it had on her daughter. I invited this woman to a ten-minute Reiki session, to demonstrate the Reiki experience. She was amazed, and agreed afterward that she could understand how profound Reiki rest functions.

Can YOU?

Our culture values **work**, not rest. We speak of the value of a "work ethic", but never mention a "play ethic". So we ignore a vital component of a complete and well-balanced human life. Rest is far more important than most people have realized. Reiki rest is the cornerstone of this book. Reiki rest provides mental and emotional benefits more quickly and easily than purely psychological talk modalities. Reiki rest releases tensions that are held in the body long after the events that created them, and those tensions lie at the root of many diseases. Consider Reiki an effective preventive measure.

Culturally we either claim to be *feeling good* in a very trivial way, or we ignore NOT feeling good, for a host of reasons. On the contrary, *feeling better* is not trivial, nor simply a matter of light-heartedness. Reiki clarifies your mind, so you can think. The ability to think clearly is needed when you have an appointment with a doctor, because you want to be able to hear what the doctor says, ask appropriate questions, and understand and remember your conversation. (It's also helpful to have a friend or partner or spouse accompany you.)

How often do you need to think clearly? It's helpful when preparing income tax returns. A clear mind collects data easily, and arranges it into helpful patterns. A clear mind can converse comfortably with people who hold opposing beliefs. Reiki assists thinking clearly.

What would life be like if we could choose to use the energy of our real feelings in productive, positive ways? A few people can and do produce prodigious results despite overwhelming challenges, without

Reiki. With Reiki, however, ALL of us can do far more than we have imagined we can.

It is a challenge to live differently. We have begun to find a more effective balance between feelings and rationality. I mean, a more effective balance is one that is sustainable – where feelings do not overwhelm rationality, nor does rationality stamp out emotions. Reiki can help us find beliefs that enhance our lives without causing harm.

This same sort of thinking can apply to human behaviors, to coping mechanisms. How sustainable is our culture if boys repress or abuse girls? Is that behavior unavoidable? Can behavior be changed? We can change our behavior when we decide to.

I believe we are free beings. I believe we make choices. Some are made rationally in consciousness. Some are chosen by default, when the free choices are replaced by habitual patterns of behavior, or set off by emotional reactions to unconscious beliefs.

Emotions can overtake us and leave us rattled instead of rational. Life is easier when you can think rationally even in emotionally trying situations. Life can be choice-filled. Using Reiki on ourselves, we can allow ourselves real emotions. We can balance reason and emotions without having to repress either.

We find, after deep Reiki rest, that we are refreshed and creative. If we continue to use Reiki, day by day our unconscious blocks melt away. Day by day, the practice of Reiki on our own self makes changes in our energetic, mental and emotional fields that open our minds to good and helpful ideas we never would have had. *Day by day* requires consistent practice, and *day by day* is much easier to manage if we treat ourselves. The practice of Reiki, simply on our own self, can become a life-changing spiritual, mental, and emotional discipline.

Do you want to feel better than you do now? Reiki can take you where you want to go. Think about it, plan for it, send Reiki to your plans and hopes. Rest in Reiki, feel your energies realign. Life becomes an exciting adventure.

You might take the example of that new Reiki practitioner whose mother sees how much she has changed. That person can be you. Reiki practitioners tend to be examples of how much more relaxed and happy we could be, how much more present and sensitive to people around them, not because Reiki-informed people have wild talents but because they practice Reiki. Giving Reiki is as good as getting it.

Reiki is a way to sanity, to a balanced and happy life. Practitioners discover wells of peace and patience they didn't have before. And – if you take as little as the first level of Reiki, you are a practitioner. A practitioner does not have to work a 40-hour week to experience its benefits. The benefits show up for people who simply treat themselves. You are a Reiki practitioner if you do Reiki for friends or close family members, and do it for free. You are a real practitioner if you simply join a Reiki-share group, or volunteer somewhere – a rehab facility, an animal rescue facility, or stand outside a cage at a zoo.

My most important point, again, is allow Reiki to flow in you. We all become accustomed to an unnecessary level of pain and stress. We put off doing what it takes to feel better (like eating right? Exercise?), because we do not usually make our own feelings a priority until we become very sick or have an accident. You can forestall your body calling for change by illness. You can motivate yourself. Allow Reiki to flow in you, to increase your motivation. You do not have to self-medicate with drugs or anything else, to feel better now.

You deserve to feel better than you do. "Just coping was all I was doing!" cries out a woman in a TV ad for a medicine. Another ad for a different medicine laments, "I knew something was missing. What was missing was ME." Coping is an automatic behavior, originally designed for one's good. Eventually one may realize that single-minded, single-reaction behavior has taken over one's life. The active, free, response-able, non-reactive, choice-making PERSON you are (and want to be always) can go missing.

You can RELEASE dysfunctional coping mechanisms that got you by for years and years, and live a well and happy, purpose-filled life.

Conclusions

In later chapters you'll find testaments to amazing results from using Reiki in a variety of situations. I'll show acceptance of Reiki as a companion to medical practice, including studies of Reiki's use in specific medical situations. But I am especially writing to tell you, **health is more than lack of disease.** We live in a soup of emotional distress, and think this is normal. I want to deepen and broaden your understanding of the stress-relieving aspect of Reiki. Life can be better.

I also want to express personal gratitude for the results of Reiki in my life that I never expected. I memorized the Kipling quotation at the head of Chapter 1 in eighth grade and recited it to the class for an assignment in English. Ever since, that has been a personal goal to reach, a transformation I wanted for my life. The result of using and giving Reiki for me has been flexibility and openness to new ideas, as well as the mental and emotional stability that I have always idealized. Inner stability and a broad perspective stand in good stead in these chaotic times.

Now, I offer myself Reiki every day, for *little things*. Life is so much better. Hands on chest, I allow Reiki to flow through me during the first snooze alarm. Then I am able to get out of bed full of energy, without all those little stiffnesses and pains and creakiness that I blamed on aging. I allow myself to enjoy Reiki when my mind is distracted by emotion. I allow Reiki to refresh me when I'm tired, mentally or physically. Now I use Reiki often, a little bit at a time.

By the way – do you think Reiki has to be applied for at least half an hour, or maybe more than that, to be effective? No way. A little bit, now and then – but not so seldom that you forget – does wonders. Keep it frequent. This works for stress in life as we live it. Ten minutes will get you going. Then five minutes later when you lose your cool the next time. Before long, you lose your cool less and less, and then you have to really THINK about when else to use Reiki, to keep it up. Go for it!

I am sprinkling these bits of advice throughout this book, instead of making a separate chapter, to refresh your awareness that Reiki can be useful to you often, throughout your day. I'm with the *more is better* crowd, and like Mrs. Takata (one of our Reiki ancestors you'll read about in Chapter 4), I extend my Reiki practice to *more OFTEN*. Giving myself Reiki frequently works for me better than limiting myself to extended sessions.

Extended sessions can be appropriate when treating many physical conditions. At the same time, Reiki treats more than the physical body as we define it. Our physical condition is not divorced from our mind and emotions. Reiki benefits our mind and our emotions every time we use it. Part of our daily stress arises because our attention is so often shifting, multitasking, and reacting to demands.

As human beings, we need to live holistically. We need to exercise mind and emotions harmoniously. We often need to regroup, i.e. to return to our personal energetic center. Giving and receiving Reiki improves our ability to live healthfully and creatively. Using Reiki for ourselves provides valuable self-care.

A patient in the specialty clinic outpatient waiting room said to me recently, after the ten-minute experience we offer there, "Why does anybody refuse this? This is WONDERFUL!"

Chapter 3

Reiki for Chronic Conditions

My newly ignited passion for Reiki sent me further than volunteering. I began to think of teaching Reiki, and mentioned my hopes to friends. One friend, nearing 90, had been a nurse, and had learned basic Reiki to use it in nursing. She connected me to a family she had known for years.

Tim

The husband, Tim (name used with permission), turned 70 during the week we worked together. He had Parkinson's, including tremors. His wife was determined to help him using non-medical means, because she believed natural methods could help without side effects. She had pursued dietary changes that seemed to benefit him, and then went on to energetic means. A Chi Gong teacher refused to try, so Reiki was the wife's next hope. Tim could stand up only with assistance, and walked stiffly and slowly, also requiring assistance. Even though movement was difficult, he needed to make the effort frequently because just sitting for a long time became painful. He could barely speak, the sounds understandable only to his family. His face was downcast and expressionless. His right-foot tremor was constant. He was so troubled by the tremor that he had refused to go to church for two years.

I suggested that both Tim and his wife take the classes and attunements for first and second level Reiki, so that he could allow himself to receive the flow of Reiki many times during each day. That would increase the amount of Reiki he could get each day. Their pre-teenaged daughters participated as well, at my suggestion, because in the family's circumstances the daughters provided care to Tim often. Their friend the nurse, who had brought us all together, also joined in, even though she had been attuned to Reiki I and II many years previously.

I prepared the first session with Distant Reiki. Tim's tremor stopped when he entered the Reiki-filled classroom.

After the Reiki I attunement, we able-bodied participants gathered around the Reiki table and gave Tim about 30 minutes of Reiki. That was 30 minutes from five people (wife, daughters, me, and our nurse friend). That night, Tim slept straight through, which had not happened for years. And he had two bowel movements during the evening, though he had been severely constipated for a long time.

The next day we were all excited. During the class for the Reiki II attunement, he was much brighter and clearly attentive. All were learning the several symbols that have special meaning in Reiki, and he managed to draw them on his own. His drawings were better than anyone's, though very slow. He was especially adept at the symbol that is actually a Chinese character, because he had been a college professor in China. The tremor in his right leg was absent all day.

We took a break for a day because the family had plans of their own. They had traveled from Houston to Bay area for our class, and wanted to look at property to relocate to, some distance away. That break day was harrowing for them because a massive traffic snarl delayed their return by several hours, on the already-three-hour trip. The stress level was high for everyone in the car that day. The tremor in Tim's leg returned.

Tim's wife had asked to go forward with the Master's level so she could offer her husband as much Reiki energy as possible. (Each level's attunement raises the intensity of energy the practitioner can emit.) It is not normal procedure to move immediately to Master level, because in many cases the students require time for the attunements to take full effect in their nervous system. Generally, students observe that during the waiting period energetic clearing occurs.

For the nurse, who had been attuned to both first and second levels years before, there might be no problem. The wife seemed to me to be completely okay to go ahead, possibly because her intent to help her husband was very clear and strong. Results for Tim had been impressive, physically, while his difficulty verbalizing made it impossible to estimate mental or emotional releases under way. I decided to go ahead for all three. The daughters found entertainment for themselves.

Rather than experiencing any hesitation about stress the class might have on the husband and wife, I found myself impressed by the husband's reactions to our continuing. The Holy Fire II Master's class in the ICRT tradition prepares students to teach Reiki (although not everyone who takes it actually does teach). Early in the first day of the Master's class, a meditation prepares the students energetically for teaching. I guided the meditation, slowly and quietly for a few minutes. Then followed a period of soft background music while each student sank into his or her respective meditative experience. I watched the dad's face change. His eyes opened wider and wider, and he began to smile, as broadly as he could. He held that expression as long as the meditation music lasted.

I understood intuitively that in his change of expression I was seeing something amazing and special. I watched him, a former university professor, experiencing the energy centers that are used in teaching being stimulated. He had not been able to teach for quite a few years. I saw wonder in his face, and delight, and it was a precious experience to me, as a former teacher myself, to be instrumental in such a profound reawakening.

At the end of the second day of Master's training, Tim seemed to marshal his energy carefully, then looked straight into my eyes and enunciated clearly, "Thank you". For someone who had been unable to speak more than whispered mutters, this too was big progress. We all were thrilled.

Two months later, in an email update, the wife informed me that her husband's tremors had gone for good. He could also walk unaided.

Do you want relief from the stresses of your condition?

I am writing this book especially to encourage all patients with a chronic condition, including chronic pain, to find a teacher of Reiki. I am not promising instant or complete healing for anyone, but it is clear to me that many symptoms can be alleviated by treatment with Reiki, in addition to drugs and other therapies.

I do not mean to generalize from one man's situation, but to use his case as an illustration. Parkinson's is a complex of symptoms, without a known single cause, and it is particularly susceptible to improvement when one uses Reiki. Whatever the cause or causes may be, Tim's case illustrates how symptoms of Parkinson's can be alleviated to some extent if one uses Reiki.

So I'm suggesting that you find a practitioner near you. You may be surprised to find how many there are. It is an easy task – type *Reiki near me* into your browser. Local practitioners will show up – at least those who have advertised their business – and some of them will also teach. Try out his or her work by paying for a session or two, and sign up for a class if the treatment satisfies you. If you are a caregiver, it is safe to encourage your loved one to allow treatment, because Reiki does not do harm, and its benefits are many.

The back-story is that both patients and caregivers need to be willing to try out, to be open to possibilities, to risk hope. Just as you do when seeking the *right* medical doctor, you always need to allow for interpersonal quirkiness. Practitioners, like doctors, are people as well as professionals.

Reiki works. You do not have to *believe in it*, for it to work. But if you refuse the energy, it cannot work in you. This is not strange – you can refuse to allow yourself to meditate, and Reiki energy is a bandwidth only a bit wider than meditation. Reiki works, just as meditation works, and like the effect of meditation on the mind, we can't fully explain or predict consequences of Reiki on our bodies – except that, the consequences are never harmful.

William Lee Rand wrote, "…since Reiki respects free will, it will not heal us or develop these higher states unless we invite it to do so. This requires that we be willing to change." (*See https://www. reiki.org/faq/historyofreiki.html,* under the heading *The Essence of Reiki,* near the end of the article titled *What is the History of Reiki*?)

Watch your expectations and demands. You probably want healing faster than it happens, for instance. I always do. Accept what you get at first and continue to pursue your long-term goal. *Slow and steady wins the race* can be true in Reiki, too. Besides, it's likely that some seeds of your chronic condition lie in your own past, meaning that what took years to build up may take some time to resolve. On the other hand, healing can also happen more quickly than you expect, so keep an open mind about that.

Anyone with any chronic condition will benefit from daily Reiki self-treatment. The reason for this is both simple and complicated. Every time we notice something isn't right, tension arises. Both body and mind react to fix it. When the condition persists, the *fix it* impulses are thwarted and frustration builds. Frustration is not a helpful tension. You may become so accustomed to your particular level of frustration that you don't notice it any more, but the tension is still part of you. The more tension you hold in your body, the less energy your body has for its regular functions and for responding to special needs.

At the very least, Reiki can eliminate those underlying tensions. Release is actually a daily need, since every day holds its own frustrations. This is one reason I recommend patients or caregivers learn Reiki themselves, so that daily treatment can be convenient. Releasing long-held tensions, frustrations and anger can require more time treating. Longer sessions with a professional practitioner can be helpful, because conversation about problems can help bring clarity and understanding. Among our predecessors in Reiki, Mrs. Takata sometimes treated a single person many times in a day, and Dr. Hayashi used multiple practitioners at a time. You'll read about both of these people in Chapter 4.

Another aspect of any chronic condition is complexity of symptoms. There can be muscular or joint aches and pains, tremor, headaches, heart palpitations, breathing problems. The mind can become confused by too many negative signals, and confusion in itself begets fearfulness, adding fear to the fear one might feel about any negative symptom. Reiki rest can relax all these fears in the mind as well as the body.

Of course, seek treatment by a Reiki professional, in addition to self-treatment. Many people are happy to share Reiki for free. But in the United States, using your browser to find a Reiki professional usually nets practitioners who expect payment. The cost of a Reiki treatment is on a scale similar to massage, in the United States. Insurance companies do not yet cover Reiki. Chiropractic has been of remarkable benefit to many people, for more than 100 years, and finally some insurers cover it. The same can happen for Reiki, when its practice becomes widespread. Any reader who ventures to try Reiki is participating in a change for the better, not only for the practice of medicine, but energetically for society and this planet. Maybe that's a worthy goal for anyone who feels his or her life has been robbed of significance by illness.

The upshot is, that a combination of self-treatment with occasional professional treatment is a practical way to achieve a more comfortable life with any chronic condition.

If you have a family member, a caregiver, or someone who tends to you frequently, adding treatment by those persons can make a huge change for the better. Anyone can practice Reiki. Ask your friends, family and caregivers to learn Reiki. The financial investment in Reiki I-II training can add immense benefit at a cost that turns out to be negligible.

At this time, the medical establishment has little awareness of Reiki or its benefits, so you can't expect your doctor to recommend it. You, if a medical consumer, need mainly to know that Reiki energy releases stress, especially subconscious tensions that are inevitable when one's health becomes a challenge.

Reiki can be safely added to any medication protocol because it has no side effects and does not interact with medications. The only contraindication for the use of Reiki shows up when you enter a new treatment regimen in which the doctor needs to observe how you react to the treatment in isolation from other factors.

If you tell your doctor about your good results, your experience with Reiki can add to the growing pool of evidence that contributes to the expansion of possibilities for positive supportive care. The more evidence we have of the usefulness of Reiki, the more likely that serious science will be generated.

It could help you to know that Reiki is really not a wild card in the medical field. The NIH (National Institutes of Health) has a branch referred to as NCCAM (National Center for Complementary and Alternative Medicine), formerly known as NCCIH (National Center for Complementary and Integrative Health).

The acronym CAM (Complementary and Alternative Medicine) occurs commonly in medical journals, and there are journals devoted to these therapies. Reiki, Therapeutic Touch, and Healing Touch are all considered to be *biofield therapies*, so you'll find the term *biofield* if you read about Reiki in medical articles. (You'll also find it in Chapter 6, Reiki for Geeks.)

Since Internet research can be haphazard, you might prefer to use PubMed®, a service of the National Library of Medicine. PubMed® contains publication information and, in most cases, brief summaries of articles from scientific and medical journals. Guidance on using PubMed® can be found on the PubMed website, *https://www.ncbi. nlm.nih.gov/pubmed.*

Reiki is not magic

This assertion has three meanings. *Not magic* means no trick is involved. Magicians do amazing feats, but we always know there was a trick to their accomplishment. There is no hidden trick involved in Reiki. Reiki is real energy, doing what it does – we might not be able to explain every result but that does not mean that results happen by accident or by fooling us.

I also mean, no malevolent spiritual force is involved. If you watch a practitioner, he or she stands behind or beside the client, and touches the client with their hands, or else hold their hands a few inches away from the client's body. The energy is not visible. There is no action, except the occasional changing of hand positions. If you believe in invisible forces that wreak havoc on people against their will, you might wonder if that could be happening. I write to assure you, that is not the case. Reiki now has science on its side.

Third, we expect that magical events are usually instantaneous. Reiki's effect seldom comes instantaneously. It is possible, but I'm not promising.

Think outside the box

You may not have a chronic condition like Parkinson's. You might have chronic back pain. Or rheumatoid arthritis. Or incomplete healing after a surgical procedure. Try Reiki.

Mike and Chellie Kammermeyer, friends of mine who are now Reiki professionals, *http://www. innercompassreiki.com*, have stories on themselves to share. (Chellie writes for Reiki News Magazine.) She writes here about her husband's experience as follows.

Mike Kammermeyer (by Chellie)

I came home, [from my first class in Reiki] like many beginning students, determined to "Heal" someone. My first client was a captive audience. My husband. Mike had grown up in Alaska. As a small child his family lived off the land and went through the process to homestead acreage. Living in the harsh environment of Alaska with a conservative family led Mike to be very cautious with his belief systems. The idea of Reiki was considered "too out there" for him to believe it would work.

Before we met, he worked on the oilrigs on the North Slope of Alaska in the Bering Sea. He had an accident, falling 20 feet and injuring his back. The result was surgery. And then follow-up surgeries, because the discs above and below the original surgery site were compromised. The month prior to my first class, he was starting to have symptoms again. His doctor was recommending he have another surgery, this time more extensive.

When I arrived home from the class, I asked him to lie on our bed and I put my hands on his back. I was spellbound at how hot they got. Mike thought I had a heating pad or something to warm my hands. I did Reiki on him for approximately 30 minutes, every day for 3 weeks. The first treatment showed significant improvement. By the end of the first week, the pain was almost gone. By the end of the second week, the pain was completely gone. By the third week, he contacted his doctor and together they determined that he no longer needed surgery.

That was 15 years ago. Since then, he has had no recurrence of pain in his back. And of course, he has also learned all the levels of Reiki, so that he can teach others too.

Other stories from Chellie appear in Chapter 5.

Reiki does not do everything

In my experience, Reiki does not grow hair on a naturally bald head (but may help grow hair back for a person who has had chemo).

For years, I have personally turned to chiropractic when a misalignment is causing pain, because manipulation is quick and easy. I ask for acupuncture when the pain is more mysterious than misalignment. In fact, when I'm in pain, it's hard to think of anything but alleviating it. I always want help to come as quickly as possible so I still go for OTC meds, then add Reiki.

People reach the end of their life as we experience it, and pass on, even though Reiki is being given to them. In a later chapter I'll recommend the use of Reiki in Hospice care to reduce stress for both patient and caregivers as well. In fact, the wonderful man with Parkinson's, who made so much progress as described already, contracted pneumonia, and after weeks in ICU, died. His wife was beside him, giving him Reiki, and I was giving Reiki at a distance.

Chapter 4

History shows us Reiki's appeal

Why look at the history of Reiki? The history of Reiki shows us that Reiki was welcomed from its very beginning, yet at the time appreciated mainly for its use for physical healing for people. (Other exciting applications of Reiki have since been developed, as you'll find in Chapter 7 and 8.)

The practice of hands-on healing seems to have been very popular in Japan in the early 20th century. The understanding at the time was that disease manifested when one's energy field became disturbed. Restoration of energetic alignment would bring back health. Many people believed that during hands-on healing, universal energy was flowing through human hands. They believed that universal energy was touching and realigning a disturbed human energy field.

In a twenty-year period, at least four people in Japan practiced hands-on healing in their own styles. One of them was Mikao Usui, whose work persisted and became the practice we know as Reiki today. The rest of them later dropped out of public view (See "What is the History of Reiki?" by William Lee Rand at *https://www.reiki.org/faq/historyofreiki.html*).

Mikao Usui

Usui was not a medical doctor. In some respects he was an ordinary person. During his lifetime he held several different positions in the Japanese government. Some material about him may be legendary, but his reputation may have included employment as a "public servant, office worker, industrialist, reporter, politician's secretary, missionary and supervisor of convicts" (See *http:// reiki.nu/history/usui/usui.html*, article titled Usui Sensei, 1865 -1926, fourth paragraph).

None of these occupations held his interest the way the pursuit of spiritual experience did. He was more a student at heart, with various interests. The passion of his life was spiritual development, starting with his spiritual root in Buddhism. He spent many years traveling to holy places and studying, including in Tibet and in the United States, where he studied the Bible and the tradition that Jesus healed by the laying-on-of hands.

He remained a Buddhist however, because he was most interested in the tradition of Enlightenment. He studied Sanskrit to understand Hindu texts on Enlightenment better. He believed that when he achieved Enlightenment, then the purpose of his life would become clear to him.

In his quest, he heard that one could achieve Enlightenment by fasting and meditating on Mt. Kurama in Japan. A famous Buddhist monastery is located there. In March 1922, Usui visited the monks, and then went off to a spot alone to conduct the requisite regimen.

He believed that immediately after this experience, he would discover the path that would express his particular way to benefit humankind.

On the 21st day of fasting and praying, the hoped-for spiritual experience occurred. Afterwards, he was so delighted that he started to run down the mountain to tell the monks. On the way, he stubbed his toe. He sat down and held the painful toe for some minutes, till the throbbing stopped. When he took his hand away, the toe was free of injury. Usui believed that he had healed the wound.

Usui realized that he had found the passion he had longed for. As promised, it had appeared after the peak experience he'd had. He was confident now that his path was to be a healer.

He opened a clinic a month later in Tokyo and began treating people as well as teaching spiritual principles. His success was immediate. He attracted attention, especially from older Japanese people who saw his work as a return to earlier values and traditions. Students also appeared and learned by assisting him.

On Sept 1, 1923, an earthquake with a magnitude of 7.9 on the Richter scale shook Tokyo. More than 140,000 people perished, and those lucky ones who were simply injured found medical facilities completely overwhelmed. Usui's clinic consequently flourished. Reiki was satisfying an urgent need for care following that environmental disaster. Everything that Reiki did was needed.

The disaster motivated Usui to attune and train practitioners, and do this quickly. He never tried to publicize his work, but those who saw the results of his practice were impressed. Usui soon saw a need to create a handbook of hand positions for his student practitioners. It was later translated into English and partially published. (More on all this appears in Chapters 6 and 7.)

When Usui died, only two and a half years later, he had attuned and trained more than 2,000 students to the first degree of Reiki so they could practice as healers. To ensure that Reiki continued, Usui also had taken 15-17 (some accounts claim as many as 20) students to the third Reiki degree that prepares them to teach and pass on the capacity to attune students of their own. An association of practitioners was also created to carry on his work. The persistence of Reiki seemed certain.

Dr. Chujiro Hayashi

Among the last of Usui's students was Dr. Chujiro Hayashi. Dr. Hayashi was the second important person to influence the practice of Reiki today. Dr. Hayashi had been trained to be a medical doctor in the Japanese Royal Navy and held a number of positions in it. At his last station before retiring, he met several people who were students of Usui. Dr. Hayashi was intrigued, and studied with Usui after his retirement.

When Dr. Hayashi was prepared to practice, Usui asked him to open a clinic of his own, and to develop Reiki scientifically. Dr. Hayashi created notebooks full of observations of the reactions of patients to hand positions used during treatment, and developed protocols - recommendations of the most effective hand positions he found for particular conditions. (Chapter 7 will tell you more about his manual.)

One of his students was Mrs. Hawayo Takata, the third in sequence of important figures for Reiki today. In 1938, Dr. Hayashi made a trip to Hawaii, to attune Hawayo Takata to Reiki Master. The trip changed his life forever, but secured the importance of his legacy.

At that time, Japan was in the throes of initiating war on its own, hoping to raise its military presence in Southeast Asia and gain access to resources that the country needed to pursue its high hopes for military and industrial prominence.

Japanese government authorities questioned Dr. Hayashi when he returned from Hawaii. The Japanese government wanted to know details about American power in Hawaii and the Pacific.

Dr. Hayashi found himself in an untenable position. He had been trained as a medical doctor in the Japanese Navy and served in it until his retirement in 1925. He was still loyal to Japan. But he was unwilling to furnish information about the US military in Hawaii because he did not want to contribute to war there. He could not compromise. On May 10, 1940 he resolved his personal conflict by an honorable Japanese tradition at the time, ritual suicide, without divulging any information he might have had about American military installations in Hawaii.

The war's aftermath greatly affected the practice of Reiki in Japan. After the war, the United States had authority over Japan. In its authority as winner of the conflict, the United States required that everyone functioning in a healing capacity in Japan become licensed in their own specialty. The United States has long had a system for licensing medical professionals, so we might expect compliance to be simple.

However, the practice of Reiki had never been licensed in Japan under its own rule, and Reiki practitioners objected to becoming subordinate to a foreign demand for a licensing system. For that reason, the practice of Reiki went underground, so to speak. Teaching Reiki also disappeared from view. Reiki virtually vanished from Japan.

Eventually, the only Reiki Master in public practice was Mrs. Takata, in Hawaii. She carried Reiki to the United States.

Mrs. Hawayo Takata

Mrs. Takata's personal story brought her into Reiki for physical healing. She was a native of Kauai, Hawaii, born there in 1900 of Japanese immigrant farm workers. She married a Japanese man who also worked on the same plantation she did, but he died in 1930. She was left with two daughters to raise, and they lived in poverty, despite her working every kind of job she could find. She became very ill from the stress of work.

When her sister died, about five years later, Hawayo visited Japan to tell her family. She believed she could find treatment in Japan for her illnesses, so she went to a hospital in Tokyo for medical diagnosis. There are several accounts of her condition, but they differ from each other in some details. In Reiki: Hawayo Takata's Story (Archedigm 1990, ISBN: 0-944135-06-04), author

Helen Haberly says that the doctor "confirmed she had a tumor, gallstones, and appendicitis" (Op.cit., p.19). (Ms. Haberly's list of complaints may not be definitive.) The doctor recommended surgery. Mrs. Takata decided against that. She had heard of a Reiki clinic she wanted to try. The doctor's sister took her there, where tumor and gallbladder problems were confirmed. Dr. Hayashi was Director of that clinic.

Mrs. Takata's treatment was given according to Dr. Hayashi's preference of using multiple practitioners at each session. In four months' time, receiving treatments twice a day, she was completely healed.

She studied under Dr. Hayashi when her treatments ended. Dr. Hayashi intended to keep Reiki in Japan, for Japanese people only. Because she was an American citizen, her application to study with Dr. Hayashi was accepted only with reservation. (Much more can be found in the little book mentioned earlier.)

Mrs. Takata practiced Reiki in Dr. Hayashi's clinic for a year, and received both first and second degrees of Reiki from him there. She returned to

Hawaii in 1937 and opened a clinic of her own. Dr. Hayashi accepted an invitation from her to visit her in Hawaii. He initiated her to Reiki Masters' level in 1938, and assisted her as she began her work. When he returned to Japan, the Japanese had not yet entered the war, and his own work took the turn described already.

Mrs. Takata changed Dr. Hayashi's treatment protocol. Instead of correlating hand positions to the healing of particular conditions, she taught a series of positions that she believed would constitute a complete general treatment. Her system began with several placements at the patient's head and proceeded along the trunk in accordance with the expectation that head and trunk contained all the energy centers believed to be important. She then added positions at the client's feet.

Thoughtful people, since she taught her system, have observed that her hand positions along the trunk avoid covering the chakras, and some people believe that such avoidance is important. Other people notice that her system actually covers all endocrine glands, and believe her effectiveness relates to improving output by those glands.

Mrs. Takata did not mention either chakras or endocrine glands in her teaching, however, as far as I know. She seems to have preferred to teach Reiki as a very simple practice, believing that Reiki would be effective even when applied by people who are not sophisticated energetically or schooled in spiritual practices. Her understanding seems to have been correct, since countless practitioners claim lineage from her and have been successful.

Practitioners now tend to combine her system with later-developed techniques such as Reiki drumming (Chapter 8), or Tibetan symbols (Chapter 9). Modern practitioners also usually follow their natural impulse to apply energy directly to painful areas. Some use Byosen scanning (more on this in Chapter 7). When you go for a Reiki session, you may encounter any one of these modifications.

It seems that Mrs. Takata absorbed the belief that *more Reiki is good* from Dr. Hayashi. Instead of using multiple practitioners in her clinic in Hawaii, she herself would treat many sessions close together. When treating at her home she would treat for a while, break while making tea, treat another while, and so forth. Sometimes she would treat for hours in a single session.

Eventually Mrs. Takata did exactly what the Japanese Masters had feared. She traveled to the mainland United States in 1970 and introduced Reiki here, principally by teaching. The result of her initiative is that the practice of Reiki survived and has flourished. Between 1970 and her death on December 11, 1980, she initiated 22 Reiki Masters.

There is no doubt that Mrs. Takata's practice and the practitioners who followed her teaching were effective, but as the practice of Reiki continued, variations sprang up. Those mentioned above may be found less commonly than the practice that makes intuitive sense – lay hands on any part that seems affected. Today, some practitioners focus on people's joints, while some focus on painful areas other than glands or joints.

What we have learned from this brief overview of the beginning of Reiki is that many people have found Reiki helpful, for many sorts of physical conditions. Reiki can be sufficient to precipitate complete healing. That has happened often enough that many hopeful people who turned to Reiki were satisfied.

Chapter 5

Confessions of a Reiki Practitioner

1. I believe in science.

I believe there are fields to investigate that we have not opened. Reiki is a new field. The experiences are real. We have not explained them. The toss-off comment, "Oh, it's all in the head," is too simple. "It's all woo-woo," begs the question, and avoids confronting the phenomena directly.

I trust *where we live.* I mean, philosophically one can argue that nothing we experience is really real, and that there is NO *out there.* But I live where *out there* IS real, in the way that word makes sense to all of us. So maybe we live where truth exists only because we agree to *what is so.* But meeting minds, coming into agreement, is a huge task for our human lives on this planet, and I accept that.

2. I believe God IS – Divine Consciousness and Source.

I also believe in spirituality, Jesus, the compassion of the Buddha, the wisdom of the Rishis, and an infinite and eternal *Cloud of Witnesses*, myself included. I make no attempt in this book to define or to reconcile all these elements into a Unified Field Theory. This book is about Reiki and how we can see it fitting into science, as we know it today.

It is clear to me that Reiki has been built into Creation as a tool to bring our perceptions back into clarity. My experience, corroborated by other people, is that healing of mental and emotional trauma feels glorious, worthy of giving thanks for.

But I also have corroboration that when one asks the Divine for healing, the result is an experience glorious beyond words, and is lasting. The *peace which passeth all understanding* is such healing.

Human engendered healing is marvelous and worthy of praise. Reiki engendered healing is glorious and creates peace. Divine healing provokes still another response. We CAN know God, and really know that we know, and all is well and worthy of praise, because all IS Divine Creation. We live in a unified Creation we have not plumbed the depths of. We trust it to continue to evolve in Divine order.

3. I like animals more than I like people.

Animals are easier to love, and you are more likely to get love back from an animal than you are from a person. Besides that, animals make the best ambassadors for Reiki. After all my effort to demonstrate the reality of Reiki, animals do it naturally. Animals can't make it up. When they are sick they respond to Reiki without thinking about it. Animals just get well.

Or, they don't respond, and die – the way people do. The way my friend with Parkinson's did.

Example of Reiki for cats

Using Reiki along with veterinary medicine is not yet common. A Reiki teacher and friend of mine, Sabine, told me about using Reiki for her cat. Sabine writes:

When I found my–then still stray–cat, he had had an accident and needed surgery in a veterinarian clinic.

After surgery he was put into a cage in a recovery room and I was allowed to spend my afternoons there. The room was full of cages holding about thirty cats in various stages between dying and recovery from surgical procedures.

Most of the time I was the only human in this room and after I had given Reiki to my cat for a while and he had signaled that it was enough for now, I went around to "ask" the other cats who wanted to be given Reiki, too (never "force" Reiki on anybody). And they all wanted and needed it… well, how do you do that with just two hands and only limited time, I asked myself. So I prayed to let me be a channel wide enough to serve them all. My inner voice advised me to stand in the center of the room and turn my palms outward.

I have no better description for what happened next than that whoever is in charge of such matters in the ethereal world pulled a throttle and converted me and my household-size Reiki-tap into a Reiki-fountain with a fire hose supply... so the cats could pull as much healing energy through me as they needed, so much that my palms became fiery hot, on fire, but in a good way. That was in no way painful, but a truly unusual experience. Have you ever seen one of those fantasy movies when energy streams out of a character?

It was not necessary anymore to hold my attention on an individual cat, the whole process went on autopilot. I, my body, my energy system, had been converted into a fully automated healing tool. And this incredible flow always stopped the very second before staff came in to do their chores and was switched back on as soon as I was alone in the room again. This went on for three afternoons. At night and during my one-hour drives I sent distance Reiki and prayed for all of them.

On my last day there, the day before I could take my cat home, I overheard two nurses talking while tending to one of the dying cats. She said: "Look at her. I would never have thought she would make it, but last night she has eaten a bit and she even used her litter box."

Was it coincidence? Is it proof for the old adage of cats' nine lives and that they have supernatural capacities to recover from incredible injuries? Would she have recovered anyway? Was the vet's treatment finally working? Or was her healing the result of Reiki and prayers? I don't know. She had been so close to death that I believe she needed all of it. And even if Reiki and prayers just played a tiny part in her recovery, they might have been the morsels that made the balance tip.

Now I use this technique when I feel helpless in a situation, when I see an accident where Red Cross is already there, when I hear about a disaster with many victims far away, or when I drive past a building, knowing that a living being suffers there – any event that touches my heart but where I cannot actually do something "materially": then I turn my palms outward and say a prayer asking to let me be a channel from which those in need can draw Reiki from, hoping to give a bit of support – healing energy for those suffering or a bit more physical energy and clarity for "material" helpers.

Naturally, there is no feedback from such situations, but I think it's like donating money; it may not be the major source of help, but helpful nonetheless – and it helps the giver, too, with the feeling of having done at least something. Remember, though, that you never force Reiki on anyone. Their higher selves will decide whether or to accept the energy. We don't simply "transfer" energy, we just give our intended recipients a "direct debit authorization." (Find contact information for Sabine on final pages of this book.)

Reiki normalizes animal behavior

I am not trying to "prove" that Reiki helps animals. I am sharing experience that it does. If your own animals never need healing, you might never have the opportunity to practice on them. You can, however, experience Reiki at work with animals if you offer your services to an animal shelter or a zoo.

This sort of work is largely as a volunteer, but it can be amazingly satisfying. You can visit an animal shelter, as many people do, to walk or feed or train animals there, but you also can volunteer giving Reiki, especially to emotionally stressed animals. Dogs, for instance, often suffer when their owner surrenders them, or when they are lost or strayed. They bark incessantly for days, or else withdraw to their bed. Either behavior makes adoption by a new family a challenge. People want a happy, well-adjusted dog, not one with a behavior problem. Normalization of the animal makes it more adoptable.

You can sit in front of their cages and beam Reiki to them. Watch for signs of change. Most barking animals calm down – after a while, at least – and come to the fence for a pat. Some lie down as close to you as they can get. The least traumatized animals may come toward you immediately. Their most common reaction is to sit and look at you through half-closed eyes, or simply curl up in what we call a "Reiki nap."

My cat, Pepper

Normalization of behavior occurred to me for my own cat, Pepper. He was a rescue, but I didn't share Reiki with him for 7 years. He was a well cat, so I never thought of sharing Reiki with him, any more than I thought of allowing it to flow in me when I was well. What would be the point? Eventually, I found the point: I realized that in a couple of respects, his behavior seemed abnormal. One questionable behavior was that he always moved away from his bowl if I approached him while he was eating from it. I wondered whether he had been mistreated early in life and was still afraid.

Another oddity was that he never made a sound. Where did that behavior come from? He was able to yowl when we were driving in the car to the vet, but around the house he didn't make a sound. He would sit at the door waiting to go out, without mewing to let me know. When I finally noticed him sitting at the door, I'd let him out. *How long does he sit without mewing?* I wondered. *Is he just unusually patient?*

One day I gave him Reiki, intending to heal this possibly neurotic behavior – and, he changed. Now he talks to me, not a lot but much more than not at all. The sounds he makes are like squeaks, rather than full-throated mews, but something is better than nothing. And he allows me to step over him while he's at his food bowl.

In a zoo, where animals are kept in cages for public viewing, the work must be done casually. Reiki practitioners can stand outside the animals' cages quietly and beam Reiki. Sometimes lions will come close to the edge of the cage, and relax. Otters play faster! The caged animals seem to like contact with Reiki's beneficial energy, even though we must never imagine their docile behavior means they are like pets simply seeking attention.

Humans normalize too

What I mean by *normalize* is the change that occurs on ordinary days when you see a friend after he or she has a rigorous day at work. Your friend's eyes are dull, face unsmiling, gaze focused on something you can't see, and the tone of voice is monotonous.

These are typical manifestations of overload and weariness. When your friend gets up after ten or fifteen minutes of Reiki rest, his or her eyes have become shiny, their voice becomes vigorous again, and physical movements are energized. You suddenly remember that you love this person. Your friend may actually tell you, "I feel great!" (OR, "I feel so relaxed"), or may just start chattering away, full of life again.

4. I want more than health, for all of us.

This is my fourth Confession. The first two were short and sweet. The third is too dear to my heart to give short shrift, even though it may not immediately serve either of my two main interests, stress relief and treatment of persons with chronic conditions. Fourth, I have a broader intent behind writing this book.

The *MORE*

When I am giving Reiki, a smile shows up and hugs my face the whole time. Remember I mentioned early in this book the feeling of *bliss* that comes to me while giving Reiki (Chapter 1)? Yes, I think I have to confess bliss. This may be an individual sort of benefit. I'm not sure anyone else feels this way, though looking at the faces of Reiki teammates as they work leads me to believe they really like giving Reiki, too.

Some would say, Reiki *raises my vibrations*. Since I'm a thinker, I notice that Reiki clarifies my thoughts. One day when Reiki was flowing through me, I discovered the meaning of a term I'd been hearing without fully grasping it. The word was *expansive*. I suddenly became aware of my own energy field, and I realized that I could make it expand by asking it to. Reiki was opening my mind to new perceptions.

There is more to life and to Reiki than physical or emotional healing. What we all want in life is *the More*. What's it *like*, the *more* in life? More money, more time, more love? I confess, my experience with Reiki is not adequate to tell you everything I want to tell you about Reiki and its benefits. I asked a friend of mine, Chellie Kammermeyer, who has practiced Reiki professionally for many years, to contribute some of her experiences to this book. (You read her story about her husband in Chapter 3.) Chellie's practice has given her the opportunity to experience effects of Reiki on her clients over a long term. (This is not like psychotherapy where you go every week. This sort of person finds Reiki helpful and comes back for more Reiki now and then.) These reports of long-term perspective show how Reiki can affect your life for the good, when you practice or experience it over a span of time.

Here are a few of my friend's descriptions of *the More*:

Chellie Kammermeyer, about herself

Reiki came into my life in a very unexpected way. I was a service manager of an auto dealership, very left brained. And at the same time, I was fascinated by metaphysical ideas, "The law of attraction" and horoscopes, especially. (I realize they are nothing alike but they were outside of my realm of "normal".)

When my son graduated from college, he wanted to purchase a Mother's Day gift for me, and as coincidence would have it, he purchased a gift certificate for me to attend a Reiki I class. As I look back I see if anyone else had thought to give me a gift like this, I would have smiled politely, said thank you and never attended. But my son was the one who bought it. So, I went. I had no idea how it would change my life or the other ripples it would create.

Now, 15 years later, I am a Licensed Reiki Master Teacher with the International Center for Reiki Training. In the meantime, Reiki has helped me with so many areas of my life I barely know where to begin.

Yet, I know the biggest help, has been my ability to move past childhood abuse and trauma. I have been able to release the trauma and it no longer affects every decision I make. Additionally, I have been able to see the bigger picture that my abuser (my stepfather) was a human who had faults and regrets. He also was instrumental in my life choices that led me down the path my life has taken.

I wouldn't trade where I am now, even if I could go back and undo some of the past. I have a practice, seeing clients and teaching students Reiki. My life is rich and full of many blessings, all of which lead back to learning Reiki.

Ed, by Chellie

When I first heard from Ed, it was a series of emails asking about Reiki. He was curious if I thought Reiki could help him and he wondered what Reiki felt like. After several emails, he decided to make an appointment. And then he promptly canceled the appointment. We went through this three times before he actually came in. He was petrified. He didn't know even why he was so nervous, but he was a wreck.

The list of things going on in his life was extensive. Probably the biggest concern was that his dad had died a few months ago. Added to that, he was the oldest son so he was responsible for his mother and siblings. He had a job that seemed to be going nowhere and his support group of friends was no longer feeling very supportive.

He was actually shaking when he lay down on the table. I had gone through all of the process telling him what he might expect or not expect. His impression of the actual Reiki session was one of profound peace. And just before the peace, he felt as if the table was shaking and he started seeing colors swirling around him. When he opened his eyes, I would have thought it was a totally different person.

He was calm and relaxed. Ed came in for several sessions over the course of a few years. During that time, he also decided to learn Reiki for himself, taking Level I & II, and then ART/Master (ART is an acronym for Advanced Reiki Training, the portion of William Rand's system that is given between Reiki II and Master) *a year later. His dead end job turned around completely. He is the manager of a company facility. His mom and siblings are supportive and excited for him. He talked with his closest friend and they mutually decided their time together had come to an end. It was not a bitter fight, just a decision they needed to go separate ways.*

He continues to come in for sessions. As he left his last session, he mentioned how afraid he was at the first one. He laughed and said, "Well, maybe I knew my world was going to completely change". Ed's outlook on life and demeanor have completely changed and he tells everyone he knows about how amazing Reiki has been for him.

Sue, by Chellie

I met Sue through mutual friends. She did contract work, called "change management". Over the years she has worked for several big companies via contract. Even knowing that a contract is going to conclude can be emotionally exhausting and draining. I met her during the end of one of these contracts.

She came in for a treatment right after the contract officially ended. The unknown of what was coming next took a toll. As I was doing Reiki on her I got a mental photo of a bowl of oatmeal. My first thought was to tell her that she needed to eat healthier. Luckily for both of us, I remembered that I had been taught to be curious and not interpret what I had seen.

After our session, I asked her what oatmeal meant to her. To my surprise, her response was, "I hate that stuff. My mother used to make it for us when I was a kid. It was runny and of course I let it get cold and I was supposed to eat it absolutely every morning. We were poor so I could never have Fruit Loops like some of my friends had." She smiled and said, "I know, Fruit Loops are not really that good for you, but that oatmeal was just awful."

We talked for a couple more minutes and then she had a look of recognition. She had eaten oatmeal for breakfast that morning. Sue had made oatmeal cookies recently and decided that the oatmeal would be a less expensive way to have a meal than something she really wanted.

She stopped on her way home and purchased a box of Fruit Loops. Within an hour of getting home, she had two offers of potential job contracts and actually was able to make a choice instead of waiting for someone else to tell her what was next.

She eventually became a Karuna Reiki® Master and followed her dream to move to a Horse Rescue Ranch. She still does contract work, but on her own terms, part time, when she feels like it. In her other time, she teaches Reiki and does Reiki on people and animals.

There is MORE to *more* than we can ever predict

Chellie's stories are about long-term Reiki results. (Contact information for Chellie and Mike can be found at the end of this book.) These stories are about people who used Reiki regularly, and as a result lived *more*. Their lives turned in new and valuable directions, without being forced by circumstance. Their stories are precious and special, and are not unusual.

Yes, I am recommending learning Reiki for the long-term benefits Reiki can have, as well as for stress relief and for the physical comfort of yourself or a loved one. Using Reiki is itself a spiritual practice that results in increased awareness on all fronts, which can lead in many creative and beneficial directions, from art and science to social reform. You could become the person you have wanted to become, and serve this generation of humanity as well as the planet, while you serve yourself and your loved ones.

Reiki releases creativity

Reiki provides a degree of rest that can significantly release out-of-the-box creativity. Rest releases creativity, by pulling attention away from the tangles we find ourselves trapped in. A full and fulfilled life exercises more in us than rational thought, and we often need to realign our many *moving parts.* Reiki assists mind-body energies to align in a more productive way. Reiki promotes realignment.

We create. Situations show up that we can manage only by being creative. By the same token, life is boring when creativity is absent, and meaningless when creativity is repressed. Our daily experience however is that creativity does not always flow, (writer's block for instance) and freedom can feel elusive even in normal conditions.

Reiki releases our creativity. When I want to write, I sit with pages of notes or a relevant book on my lap, place my hands on the papers or book, and intend Reiki to flow. My hands begin to tingle. I believe that the energies in my body and chakras are coming into alignment, and that a result of this alignment is order and clarity in my thoughts. In a few minutes, the urge to write shows up, a live idea appears.

People who practice Reiki regularly become relaxed and happier people. Since there have been plenty of morose musicians, artists and poets, we can't explain that wellness is the only foundation for creativity. It is not surprising, however, that creativity can result from the release of energy held in bondage to dysfunctional behavior patterns and unsolved problems.

Solving problems is creative work

When this chapter began, I focused on *internal* problems. Reiki works not only to untangle our personal thinking process. It also relaxes our attachment to our usual perspective on the outside world. We are able to see situations freshly and find new solutions.

Historically, the usual way to achieve a new perspective is to put the problem aside for a while. How many times has a brilliant thought come to you when you were in the shower? Some people wake from a restful sleep, full of their answer. Some scientists wash test tubes for a while. It seems that in all these cases, *rest* of some sort is the operant method. Not that we can predict that a solution will show up after any particular nap. But, "Give it a rest, Charlie!" is definitely in play.

Release from the problem, relaxation of focus on a problem, allows the fertile mind to return to its natural state of creativity. Give it a Reiki rest.

Reiki release can extend to play

Satisfying life is usually not all work. We crave play, and limit play at the same time. The term *workaholic* refers to people who are dysfunctional at play. If I weren't so devoted to work on this book, I'd intend Reiki to flow in me right now, with the intent to release energy to play.

I've had experiences that suggest Reiki could stimulate our *play* muscle. My cat provided an example. I've been concerned about him for years because he does not play. Only light excites his interest – a flashlight in the dark, or reflected light from mirrors or glasses casting bright movements on the carpet when the sun falls on the lenses right.

A morning came when, after I gave myself Reiki to perk myself up, my cat sitting in my lap, I casually gave Reiki to him too, intending that he live his best life. His behavior changed. He began to take interest in a small toy available for months on the living room floor. His attention to it was erratic, but it was more play than ever before.

Shortly afterwards, I stopped into a pet store to look at cat toys – again, even though I had tried all sort of things. I found two squeaky mice. He went wild with them. He batted one downstairs and played there as well. Boredom seemed to set in again after a couple of weeks – I thought – but then I found him playing with one of the mice at night, in the dark.

How many of you out there also never play? Can you imagine how it feels, to play? If you can imagine it, is there something inside you – a belief, or an experience – that holds you back from play? (I would not know to ask, if I had not been there.) Could you try the deep relaxation of Reiki, with the intent to release the memory of the day when a parent told you stop playing and do something constructive? Or whatever other idea or belief could be at root?

We all can have a better life than we do. Reiki is a helpful tool.

Chapter 6

Reiki for Geeks

The term Geeks is slang for people who know a lot of technical data. I'm applying it to people who study the chemistry or physics of medicine. These are people who are detail-oriented and employ rigorous habits of scientific investigation. Their standards are high. They include practicing physicians and medical research scientists. Nurses can fall into this category. Count yourself *in* if you want to.

My intent is to show that Reiki can be described, at least partially, by today's scientific language. I hope to convince people that Reiki is real energy and some of its behavior can be discussed in terms that have begun to be used in science during the last few decades. Yet, even as I verbalize my suggestions, it is clear that Reiki's effects and processes are far from being completely describable in the science of today.

The practice of Reiki includes many puzzling aspects that will challenge us for some time. The prominent downside to trying to create a science of Reiki now is that we need to learn so much more about human beings in the first place - human chemistry, physics, biology, psychology – before we can understand how Reiki functions in the human being.

My work in this book is not trying to produce a complete theory, or a hard-and-fast theory. This is a sketch of a vision, rather than a proof.

One major objection to creating a science of Reiki has been that reports by individuals of their personal perceptions have been our starting point. If we are limited to personal perceptions for our data, we could easily fall for the easiest explanation of results of Reiki, namely the *placebo effect*. A placebo is an inert substance given to a person in place of a substance which can actually have an effect on that person. Experiments have shown that when a person **believes** a treatment will help, a physical change for the better can occur. This observation leads to the conclusion, "Oh, it's all in your head."

Science has expected that facts must be independent of the human observer. My speculations, based on being able to measure Reiki in terms of frequency (Hertz), could provide a solid ground to begin a science, to the extent that frequency is a measurement independent of the human observer.

I'd like to remind you that aspirin was used because it was effective – for 70 years – before its effects were understood.

A real physical process is going on, however. There is a widely-cited experiment using mice by researchers William F. Bengston and David Krinsley that demonstrates that Reiki produces real results. Bengston obtained five mice that had a type of breast cancer implanted in them by a disinterested professor of biology. Their cancer was already known to cause death between 14 and 27 days, 100% of the time. Bengston, who had been attuned to Reiki, "placed his hands around the outside of a standard laboratory plastic cage containing six mice for 1(sic) hour per day while applying the healing technique ... six control mice were kept in a separate laboratory." Bengston and Krinsley published their report on this work as The Effect of the "Laying On of Hands"(sic) in Transplanted Breast Cancer in Mice, Journal of Science Exploration, 2000; 14:353-364. (p 357). This report can be found on the Internet, complete with page numbers, at: *https://www. scientificexploration.org/docs/14/jse_14_3_bengston. pdf*. Bengston treated the mice with Reiki for 30 days. They did not die. "About 10 days into the procedure, the experimental mice began to develop a "blackened area" (sic) on their tumors" (p. 356, Op. cit.) The tumors then ulcerated and closed, and the mice lived on to a normal lifespan. The report provides convincing documentation by including numerous photographs of the mice and the progress of their tumors.

Yes, that was a very small sample, and the subjects were mice, not people. But the mice were real living animals, and the experiment was replicated three times, in different cities. In totality of the three studies, 87.9% of the energy-treated mice survived their cancer episode. All of the control mice died of their cancer.

Further, some of the mice that survived were re-injected with cancer cells, and the cancer did not "take". Bengston concluded that an immune response in the mice had been stimulated by the Reiki energy. It's his conclusion – perhaps an immune response is involved – that especially interests me.

Discovery in Japan

Can we use modern science to understand the origin of Reiki? The following paragraphs focus on specific scientific aspects of the development of Reiki, rather than on history per se as given in Chapter 4.

Mikao Usui

As stated in Chapter 1, the practice of hands-on healing gained popularity in Japan early in the 1900s. Four different practitioners were already engaged in it, when Mikao Usui, who originated Reiki as we know it today, discovered it. We know little about any of them – neither how they made their discovery, nor how their methods of treatment may have differed from Usui's. Rather than answers, we gain questions.

Our knowledge of Usui's life is also scant, but we do have an account of how he found Reiki. As described in Chapter 1, Usui was fasting and meditating, with the purpose of achieving enlightenment. He believed he reached that state, and within hours realized he also had acquired an ability to heal, based on his experience of healing his own injured toe.

I want to ask, "How did meditation result in his ability to do Reiki?" Now that we have measured the energy, and notice that the bandwidth for meditation is part of the Reiki bandwidth, we can suppose that Usui somehow reached an intensity of meditation that the Reiki bandwidth as a whole was activated in him. This is not an explanation, of course, only a suggestion that occurs to me. (Hold on, another idea is coming up.)

Other questions may have clearer scientific answers. Can we describe the change in Usui scientifically? How does Reiki energy function?

I ask, beyond the felt awareness of relaxation – what happens energetically? I am about to lead you out of my consideration of history for a look into recent scientific developments. We'll return to history, however, and bring you up to the present along a chain of datable scientific discoveries.

Usui entered a self-induced altered state of consciousness (we might say). What is that, energetically?

I am supposing that our apparently physical structure is ultimately a complex bundle of energies. I expect that every *state of consciousness* is a structure of energies. (I am supposing that some structures are simple, while others resemble a dust bunny – mainly because we ourselves sometimes realize that we are holding ideas that are confused.) I propose that Usui's normal magnetic field was altered by his long-term meditation and fasting.

Perhaps his altered condition intensified Reiki energy already flowing through him. Perhaps the altered state created a new neural pattern that gave Usui the ability to emit Reiki intentionally. Perhaps the new pathway was sufficiently stable to persist, so that he never lost the ability to do Reiki.

Or, could it be that the change in him was epigenetic? That is, the altered energy flow turned on a gene that had always been there, a gene that opens the ability to radiate extra-low-frequency energy from our hands (as we readily feel ourselves radiate heat).

Such a gene has not been identified at this time, so this is speculation. But I personally am excited to see how epigenetics might help us understand the action of Reiki.

Epigenetics

Epigenetics has been described as the Science of Change. It focuses on the fact that at least some bits of DNA code can *express themselves* or not. When they are not expressed, those genes are described as *silenced*. Why are some genes *silenced*? Why do some activate (express)? Environmental factors seem to be key.

So, perhaps the intensity of the meditation bandwidth magnified Reiki energy already present in Usui's body to the point that the expression of a gene for healing flipped to *on* and his body could then emit the Reiki bandwidth.

To give you an example of the effect of genetic expression, at the University of Georgia a recent study isolated a gene that seems to relate to social behavior. The study showed that when the gene (OXT) is turned off, its person could be less sociable than people whose gene is turned on.[2]

---

2   Proceedings of the National Academy of Sciences, reported in
    [*https://www.whatisepigenetics.com*]

I am suggesting that in Usui, the gene for ability to emit Reiki was turned on by his energetic condition at the time of his peak experience while meditating.

Neuroplasticity

Neuroplasticity is another recent field developed to describe some human behavior. The basic idea of neuroplasticity is simple. Cells in the nervous system throughout the body interconnect with each other by means of synapses. Those are points of connection, neuron to neuron, across which a tiny chemical or electrical signal passes. This is the way signals are transmitted from sense organs to the brain, and from the brain to efferent cells, i.e. muscles generating purposive movement. Synapses are communication structures. Neuron connections are not fixed. Each neuron can connect to many others, and the pathways change according to frequency of use, and experiences.

When any pathway is used frequently, it becomes relatively stronger. To quote a colloquialism, "neurons that fire together, wire together". On the other hand, the collection (neurons that "fire together") can change when experiences occur that introduce inconsistent data. (This, on a cellular level, is the same process we human beings undergo when our theories meet counter-examples.)

This bit of theory is helpful in solving the challenge of brain injury. There are recent experiments which are easily found on the internet (suggestions for research footnoted below) that show people have the ability to "remap"[3] the brain's cortical activity. Remapping is very important to people who have suffered brain-injury. There is now reasonable evidence that such disabled people can regain abilities that were lost.

In the transformational environment, it is common to describe this process as *re-wiring*. I propose that Reiki can facilitate *re-wiring* the brain. I believe that Reiki promotes re-patterning of neural pathways by relaxing habitual patterns. I believe that re-wiring in the brain is the same process that occurs when

---

3 Every part of the body is connected to a part of the brain. One can describe the result as a "cortical map." When a body part is amputated, or when brain tissue is injured by accident or internal change such as a stroke, new connections must be established, or else abilities are lost. Recent studies show that remapping is more easily done than we had previously thought. A quick search in your browser on "brain remapping" will turn up readable articles on many different circumstances in which remapping occurs in.

habitual patterns of thought are changed. The profound rest – the Extra-Low-Frequency energy that is part of Reiki sessions – is the change agent. I see the possibility that Reiki can be a very helpful tool during any process one uses in therapy to stimulate the brain to re-pattern itself. Experiments in this area have not come to my attention, but I do believe that adding Reiki to treatments for PTSD and to brain-injury rehabilitation efforts will prove very useful.

Entrainment (first mentioned in Chapter 2)

The theory of entrainment is not new. A famous example of entrainment occurred in 1656. Dutch scientist Christian Huygens was working on a design for a pendulum clock. He placed two pendulum clocks side-by-side on a wall and found that the two clocks slowly synchronized.

The concept of entrainment occurs in many areas of science today, and it is well established in the study of brainwaves. Neurons in the brain emit electrical impulses. One might suppose that every neuron is *on its own* so to speak, and the result would be a cloud of pulses occurring at different tiny intervals.

Brain activity could look energetically like a cloud of dust, chaos. Our measuring devices, however, detect accumulations of synchronous wavelengths, and the proportion of accumulations can vary from area to area of the brain.

It is said that synchronous accumulations of any wavelengths are the physical manifestation of thoughts, ideas and behaviors. This cannot be demonstrated in detail at this time. We are able to chart, in general, that slower brainwaves are dominant when we feel tired, dreamy, or meditative. When we are awake, mid-length waves dominate. When frequencies are high, we may feel *wired*, hyper-alert.

Brainwave entrainment

The brain exhibits a behavior called the Frequency Following Response. That means, under certain conditions, the brain's electrical activity organizes itself in synchronicity with external stimulations. "Music hath charms to soothe a savage beast," (William Congreve).

"Any stable frequency evokes a cortical response. The brain synchronizes its dominant brainwave frequency with that of the external stimulus."[4] Reiki is a stable frequency bandwidth, the bandwidth of meditation. Reiki energy provokes a cortical response of meditation, which is perceived as relaxation.

By the way, we may expect that only sound can be strong enough and regular enough to entrain the brain, but pulsing light entrains the brain, and so do electromagnetic fields. If a person who is subject to seizures is stimulated by a strobe light flashing at his or her seizure frequency, the person's brain will entrain to the light, and the person then will have a seizure. (Do not try this at home; the response can be very sudden and also severe.)

Dr. Chujiro Hayashi

Back to early Reiki history. Dr. Hayashi's contribution to the science of Reiki is our main consideration here.

---

4   *https://brainworksneurotherapy.com/what-brainwave-entrainment*

His medical education honed his scientific mind. He insisted on the use of Byosen, which finds empirical evidence of physical disturbance by means of refined sensory perception (Chapter 7). He hypothesized that correlations could be found between hand placements on the body, and treatment results. He kept careful records and established protocols for the treatment of a wide variety of conditions. His notes are available even today, although the thought that Reiki-action might be controlled by hand positions is no longer held by every practitioner. Dr. Hayashi's most lasting contribution has been the expectation that Reiki is a natural phenomenon that can be understood.

Mrs. Hawayo Takata

Mrs. Takata was the third major figure in Reiki as we practice it today.

Her contribution to Reiki is mainly as a teacher. Her work impinges on science by raising questions about the relationship of technique to result. Her system of hand positions covers the seven major endocrine glands of the body – pituitary, hypothalamus and pineal glands in the head; thyroid and parathyroid glands in the neck; pancreas, adrenals, and gonads (testes and ovaries) in lower trunk. There is no information about her which suggests she had Western medical education of any kind. Was this an accident, or was she following her intuition about where to place her hands?

One might expect that Mrs. Takata's style of treatment could be particularly useful to people whose problems relate to endocrine functioning. The endocrines certainly are involved in a wide variety of complaints, so there are many possibilities to study.

Scientific notice of Reiki begins

In 1939, a Russian scientist and inventor named Semyon Kirlian succeeded in exposing a photographic plate with energy coming from human fingertips. He separately exposed that same hand when radiating Reiki. On the second photographic plate, besides the white circles around the fingertips, there was a broad fan of exposure originating at the palm of the hand.

This was news. To Reiki practitioners, this was a tantalizing glimpse of Reiki as real energy. To scientists, Kirlian's work had produced evidence for the existence of Reiki, separate from the intervention of a human's introspective report. Kirlian's achievement was virtually ignored by science for 20 years. His demonstration of the factuality of Reiki finally began to receive widespread attention in the United States in the 1960s.

"I Sing the Body Electric"

This is the title of a short story and a subsequent collection of short stories by Ray Bradbury (See Bantam Books First Edition 1971, ISBN: 978-0552087858). The title seems significant in the light of the many scientific developments relevant to Reiki during the 60s and 70s.

Medicine and the human electrical field

Since the 1920s, Western medicine has routinely measured the electrical field generated by the brain using an EEG (electroencephalogram) to diagnose some medical conditions. Likewise, medicine has used the ECG (electrocardiogram, aka EKG) to diagnose heart conditions. More recently, MRI (magnetic resonance imaging) technology uses the human magnetic field to generate pictures of organs.

These developments are based on the fact that every cell in the human body produces a positive electrical charge outside the cell wall, and a negative charge on the inner cell wall. Electrical charges produce magnetic fields.

Research into the human magnetic field expanded during the 60s. The first device capable of measuring such very subtle bioenergies was a superconducting quantum interference device (SQUID). A SQUID is a magnetometer. It measures very subtle magnetic fields. The SQUID seemed therefore ideal to measure Reiki energy.

The first person to claim success may have been Dr. John Zimmerman, in the 1980s. He reported a study using a small number of Healing Touch practitioners (a technique similar to Reiki) in which a SQUID was used and showed measurements in Hertz, (0.3 – 30 Hz) which is a measure of **frequency**. Although Dr. Zimmerman's results have been widely cited, a copy of his study does not seem to exist on the Internet. You could consult, for example, a report in the article Introduction to Frequency, Electromagnetic Therapy & Pulsed Electromagnetic Field Therapy, at *http://www.pemft. org/part-2-frequency.html*. You'll find very similar wording in most citations.

Science could move in some other direction. There is an aspect of energy that we refer to in normal conversation and is also a scientific measure. The word is **intensity**. For beginners in Reiki, let me explain that practitioners often compare experiences by using the word **intensity**. Some people have believed that Reiki energy is more intense than other energy coming from a person's hands, and this belief led to attempts to measure its intensity.

The term **Gauss** is used for measuring intensity. There have been two studies in Japan, one published in 1992 and one in 1996, that used a gradiometer, and both found high intensity fields coming from energy practitioners.

An abstract of the study published in 1992, in English, can be found in PubMed at *https://www.ncbi.nlm.nih.gov/pubmed/1353653*. Its title is Detection of Extraordinary Biomagnetic Field Strength... and its authors are Seto A, Nakazato S, Hisamitsu T et al. A subsequent study, by four of the same people plus a few corroborated those magnetic field intensity findings. An abstract in English can be found also in PubMed, at *https://www.ncbi.nlm.nih.gov/pubmed/9051169*, Emission of Extremely Strong Magnetic Fields... by Hisamitsu T, Seto A, Nakato S, et al.

On the contrary, there was a 2013 study that did NOT detect high electromagnetic field intensities from the hands of several Reiki Masters. This study was conducted by Dr. Ann Baldwin, in cooperation with William Lee Rand, my teacher and herein oft-quoted author. There are two key differences – and strengths - in Dr. Baldwin's study, compared to the Japanese studies. One was that she used a SQUID, which is a much more sensitive device than the magnetometer used in the Japanese studies. A second important difference in her technique was her use of adequate shielding from outside sources of magnetic radiation. You can read her report at *https://www.liebertpub.com/action/doSearch?SeriesKey =acm&AllField=Practicing+Reiki+doe+not.*

Science – or fiction?

The weakness of science around Reiki is very clear here – there are very few studies on these basic topics bringing Reiki into the purview of modern science, and the studies used very small populations of subjects. Science is its own critic: rigorous science demands more studies, on larger fields of subjects. I expect that studies of both Gauss and Hertz measurements will eventually be replicated sufficiently to solidify our theories. At present I am offering intriguing suggestions.

Meanwhile, however, the importance of extra-low frequencies does show up, remarkably in the ultra-conservative FDA (Food and Drug Administration arm of the American Federal government). The FDA has gradually investigated and approved devices that use machine-generated extra-low frequencies to assist healing particular conditions.

PEMF devices

Scientists have been more comfortable experimenting with machine-generated frequencies than with those generated by human beings. Researchers created PEMF[5] (Pulsing Electromagnetic Field) devices that successfully imitated the pulsing Reiki energy emitted from human beings.

Machine-generated 7-Hertz energy was found to stimulate bone growth, and the FDA in 1979 approved a PEMF device to assist in cases where bone regrowth had been problematic.

As measuring abilities increased, new applications of low-frequency energies were tested, and FDA approval was granted to a number of devices. Specific Hertz (Hz) levels were found to pertain to other particular types of healing. Besides the

---

5   The use of PEMF devices to aid in knitting bones was the first Low Frequency use to earn FDA approval. Curing cancer is not yet that simple. In 2011, the FDA approved the use of PEMF devices as a supplemental measure to aid in treating brain cancer.

7-Hertz level effective in promoting bone growth, scientists found that the 2-Hertz wavelength stimulates nerve regeneration, 10 Hz stimulates ligament repair, and 15 Hz aids capillary formation. This data has become general knowledge, so you'll be able to find plenty of articles on the Internet, as well as in medical publications.

The history of FDA approval of PEMF devices shows real progress in acceptance by medicine that extremely low-frequency (ELF) electric and magnetic fields can be effective in treatment of health issues. After the first use aiding bones' knitting in 1979 came approval of five more PEMF devices for treating specific conditions:

1987 – treatment of post-operative swelling and pain,

2004 – treatment of post-operative cervical fusion,

2008 – treatment of depression,

2011 – treatment of brain cancer,

2013 – treatment of migraine headaches resistant to medication.

This is a slow but precise demonstration that science can, in fact, confirm the efficacy of low frequency energies.

Clinical developments in brief overview

Resistance to Reiki from scientific circles has diminished in recent years due to the fact that clinical uses have been developed in several areas of medicine, and recently studies have been constructed carefully enough to publish findings in clinical journals.

Hospitals and nursing facilities can create the controlled conditions under which data can be monitored and recorded. The result is a bank of information much greater than Dr. Hayashi could produce in his clinic. Studies are still weak in regard to strict requirements for thorough research, such as *blinding*.[6] Sample sizes for many reasons have been small. However, awareness

---

6   "Double blind" studies have long been the ideal in science. The term means that the study is set up so that no information is available to either the subjects or the control group that might affect their behavior. This sort of study is especially difficult to create in the study of Reiki, when results depend on reports by the persons receiving Reiki.

of the need for controls is increasing the effort to achieve reliable data.

Medicine has so far generated studies of the use of Reiki in only a few areas. Each study necessarily has its own particular agenda, which limits the studies' results. (I'm guessing that since funds for research are limited, that could also affect how seldom Reiki research is done.) The upside is that data is more reliable; while the downside is that each study covers such a small field of people and symptoms that our knowledge in any field of treatment is still appallingly small.

Pain management

Medicine is interested particularly in pain management. PEMF (Pulsed Electromagnetic Field) devices, mentioned above, entered the consumer market 20 years after their development for research in the 60s. Device developers claimed significant pain reduction in many sorts of situations and conditions. In the midst of controversy over their efficacy, Dr. Oz featured the use of PEMF devices on his TV show in 2013.

Reiki supplies the same frequencies in pulsed fashion that imitative medical devices emit. Why should people distrust results of Reiki used for pain reduction, or expect Reiki to do its work faster or more completely than the machines?

Opioids satisfy medical consumers by managing pain more quickly than either machines or Reiki. We risk addiction. Reiki offers a complementary method to handle pain. When Reiki reduces pain sufficiently, opioids may be needed much less frequently. The medical world began publishing papers with its positive findings about the use of biofield therapies to alleviate pain early in this century – though of course still in limited numbers.[7] [8] [9]

---

7   Psychological, rehabilitative, and integrative therapies for cancer pain, in UpToDate, 2017, by E. Alessandra Strada, PhD, MSCP, FT, and Russell K. Portenoy

8   Biofield Therapies and Cancer-Related Symptoms: A Review, 2014, in Clinical Journal of Oncology Nursing, Vol18, Number 5, pp. 568-576, by Silvia Gonella, MSc, RN, Lorenzo Garrino, MSc, RN, and Valerio Dimonte, MSc, RN

9   Reiki's effect on patients with total knee arthroplasty: A pilot study in Nursing, 2016, Vol. 46, No. 2), by Barbara Byrne Notte, BSN, RN, HN-BC; Carol Fazzini, RN, C; and Ruth A. Mooney, PhD, MN, RN-BC

The short story is, there are significant results when we use Reiki for pain management, especially in cancer treatment and in post-operative care.

Medical treatment of emotional conditions

I've recently begun to hear an assertion that healing is complete when it occurs at a cellular level, meaning, in the tiniest structures we know to be involved. Yes, I am claiming that during the profound rest achieved by Reiki, emotional tensions can be released at a cellular level. That possibility fuels my suggestion that people who need emotional healing will be well-served if they seek professional help that includes Reiki.

Science can do much more than it has, to treat emotional conditions medically. Nevertheless Reiki has begun to be added at treatment facilities to medical management of psychological conditions. Benefits in treating anxiety and depression appear in the forefront now.[10] [11]

10 Reiki for Depression and Anxiety (Review), 2015, Cochrane Library, Issue 4, by Joyce J. Herbison, GP

11 Effect of Reiki Therapy on Pain and Anxiety in Adults: An In-Depth Literature Review of Randomized Trials with Effect Size

Formal studies of Reiki's use by caregivers have been reported as well.[12]

Could doctors reasonably suggest Reiki to patients whose stress level is of the garden variety? Yes, Reiki could be used as a health-maintenance measure for people who think their needs are ordinary. Realistically, the garden of stressful situations is growing lush and full these days, so using whatever works – safely – is reasonable. And Reiki should certainly be considered before turning to addictive substances. This is an area in which doctors become educators, and proponents of humanly sustainable practices.

Reiki as a tool for caregivers

In Chapter 3, I recommend that spouse or siblings or even minor children train in Reiki in order to

---

Calculations, 2014, in Pain Management Nursing, Vol. 15, No. 4 (December), pp 897-908, by Susan Thrane, RN MSN OCN and Susan M. Cohen, PhD, APRN, FAAN

12   Reiki Reduces Burnout Among Community Mental Health Clinicians in The Journal of Alternative and Complementary Medicine, 2015, Vol. 21, Number 8, pp. 489-495, by Renee M. Rosada, PsyD; Beverly Rubik, PhD; Barbara Mainguy, MA; Julie Plummer, BSN, RN; and Lewis Mehl-Madrona, MD, PhD

assist family members with chronic conditions because Reiki decreases stress so profoundly. Chronic patients might not have the physical energy or financial resources to seek professional Reiki on a daily basis, but they should not fail to receive Reiki's benefits for such simple reasons. Especially pertinent to my purposes is a study of parents and caregivers who successfully trained in basic Reiki in order to share Reiki with their hospitalized children.[13] This study supports my earlier suggestion that often a close family member is in the best position to give frequent short treatments to a person with a chronic condition, or an acute condition that continues for some time, or recurs.

Reiki for quality end-of-life care

Another recent extension of Reiki into medicine is its use in hospice care. Members of the hospice team certainly provide end-of-life comfort, and Reiki can be a very helpful addition (an example

---

13 Reiki training for caregivers of hospitalized pediatric patients: A pilot program, in Complementary Therapies in Clinical Practice, 2013, Vol. 19, pp. 50-54, by Anjana Kundu, Rebecca Dolan-Oves, Martha A. Dimmers, Cara B. Towle, and Ardith Z. Doorenbos

follows in Chapter 8). Reiki provides gentle pain and anxiety relief. It's my hope that much more attention is paid to end-of-life care, and certainly that can occur as more people learn Reiki and experience its value.[14]

Conclusions

I am not in the business of proving anything, so my *conclusions* are not *therefores*. One of my intentions is to raise awareness of Reiki, and increase confidence in it as complementary to the medical arena. This chapter is intended to raise confidence for medical professionals, so that medical consumers need not hide their interest in adding Reiki. I believe that this chapter does succeed in demonstrating that the movement of science has already tended to support the use of Reiki, and medical institutions have begun to use it successfully, even though the

---

14 Biofield Therapies for Symptom Management in Palliative and End-of-Life Care, in American Journal of Hospice & Palliative Medicine, 2015, Vol. 32, pp. 90-100, by Ashley M. Henneghan, RN, BSN and Rosa N. Schnyer, DAOM, Lac

science of Reiki is not yet rigorous. The worlds of science and medicine can come together and find Reiki acceptable.

Chapter 7

How is Reiki learned? What happens when it is taught?

In Chapter 6, I wrote:
Usui entered a self-induced altered state of consciousness (we might say). What is that, energetically?

I am supposing that our apparently physical structure is ultimately a complex bundle of energies. I expect that every state of consciousness *is a structure of energies. (I am supposing that some structures are simple, while others resemble a dust bunny – mainly because we ourselves sometimes realize that we are holding ideas that are confused.) I propose that Usui's normal magnetic field was altered by his long-term meditation and fasting.*

Perhaps his altered condition intensified Reiki energy already flowing through him. Perhaps the altered state created a new neural pattern that gave Usui the ability to emit Reiki intentionally. Perhaps the new pathway was sufficiently stable to persist, so that he never lost the ability to do Reiki.

Or, could it be that the change in him was epigenetic? That is, the altered energy flow turned on a gene that had always been there, a gene that opens the ability to radiate extra-low-frequency energy (as we readily feel ourselves radiate heat).

The latter possibility is consistent with the fact that there have always been people who could heal; in the past they have sometimes viewed their ability as a gift from God. In my line of thought, *giftness* could still be true, and an example of *greater things than these* – where healing can also be seen to be part of natural creation. I believe that Usui's meditative state was strong enough to entrain Reiki energy in other people such that healing occurred for them.

Usui did not learn Reiki. He discovered Reiki, by means of his newfound ability to heal people. Energy healing already existed in Japan. According to William Rand, at least four other people in Japan by 1920 were practicing what seemed to be the same ability. As their time and culture explained it, their ability connected the human life force (Chi or Ki) in individuals to a universal energy that healed them.

Usui opened his first clinic only a month after his big change occurred. People were attracted to his work, and of course some people wanted to learn. *How could it be possible to teach Reiki, when it was a product of discovery, not learning?*

Usui's first students believed that they *caught* the ability as one would catch a cold, by proximity to the great man. It actually makes scientific sense to say that his energy field – or at least, the Reiki bandwidth part of his field – had become so strong that Reiki in him could entrain (see discussion at chapter end) other people's energy field, and flip their healing gene to *on*.

Records of those early days are sparse. The most obvious, but incomplete, source of information is carved onto a large memorial stone set up by some of Usui's followers after his death. According to William Lee Rand, there are also records in Japanese stored at the Usui Reiki Ryoho Gakkai (Ryoho means Healing Method, Gakkai means Society). This society was founded early on by Usui to carry on his work. It continued to exist during the post-war period of American occupation when Reiki virtually vanished from public view. It still exists today.

Usui believed the change had happened to him because he had for many years carefully cultivated his own inner energetic state, which we could call his *spirituality*. He encouraged his students to cultivate spiritual disciplines, too, even after they began to practice Reiki.

Western culture has devised many ways to cultivate spirituality. One method is the insight method, using holy texts. One method is meditation, achieved in many different ways. Usui also taught the use of behavioral discipline. He adapted five principles of spiritual behavior from Buddhist sources, which became known as the Five Reiki Precepts:

"For Today Only:
Do not Anger
Do not Worry
Be Humble
Be Honest in Your Work
Be Compassionate to Yourself and Others"

(translation from The Reiki Sourcebook by Bronwen and Frans Stiene, ISBN-13: 978 1 84694 181 8. Rev. 2008, O Books, John Hunt Publ. Ltd, UK). (See also the website of International House of Reiki, *http://ihreiki.com/reiki_info/five_elements_of_reiki/ reiki_precepts/*).

Training Reiki Practitioners

As written earlier, the great earthquake that destroyed Tokyo in September 1923 occurred a year and a few months after Usui had set up his clinic. Tending to the thousands of injured people created a need to multiply practitioners quickly.

Initially students thought that merely standing in the great man's presence gave them the ability to do Reiki. This could certainly have been the case if Usui's own field was strong enough to entrain their field, and kick a gene for healing to its *on* expression. He encouraged all students to be attuned many times. But Usui needed practitioners he had trained to be able to train others as well. Ultimately, he did not rely on the strength of their energetic state. Eventually he designed a ritual, a series of steps – movements, gestures, symbols, touches, and prayers – to be carried out while moving slowly around each student. Something worked. His students could indeed pass on Reiki ability.

Usui established a series of levels of ability to do Reiki. His first level students were allowed to practice Reiki on patients, but Usui believed the first level worked only with the physical body. At the second level of attunement, students were taught several symbols (see discussion later) that focus energy in more subtle ways. Third level students were prepared to teach and to attune others. Usui used terms in Japanese for each level: Shoden (first teachings), Okuden (inner teachings) and Shinpiden (mystery teachings). In the United States we tend to say Reiki I, Reiki II and Master (some people say Reiki III).

Passing on the ability to practice Reiki became routine. It was clear that Usui's Master's students were able to bring their own students to the same energetic level. Reiki students could be confident in their ability.

Learning Reiki

Learning Reiki is not like learning multiplication tables. Memorization is needed only for symbols in Reiki II and Master, not at all in Reiki I. This means that acquiring the ability is much easier than you might have thought. Almost anybody can acquire the ability to do Reiki.

You will encounter various terms for what is happening. The first word in Japanese to refer to attunement seems to have been *reiju*, which referred to the experience a student could have, standing near a great Master and absorbing his energy. In time, the term became *attunement* in English.

After attunement, students always have the ability to use Reiki. Some people emphasize that Reiki energy never changes. Since Reiki has been found to be a definite frequency range, in that sense the energy never changes.

But Usui believed that Reiki energy emitted by any person could be made *stronger*. That may have come from his observation of students. It may be a reason for his practice of attuning students multiple times. It may also explain why he encouraged students to continue their individual spiritual disciplines. My observation of myself does confirm that the mental and emotional practices we use to clear our own inner contradictions does affect my personal energy, so I presume that the Reiki energy I channel may also become stronger, as I develop personally. Furthermore, Usui believed that students should attain a certain level of spiritual or energetic strength in order to receive the next level of Reiki.

At the Reiki II level, Usui taught the use of symbols to refine Reiki energy.

What are symbols?

Reiki I students are given the ability to access and apply Reiki energy simply by intention. Advanced Reiki practitioners, however, learn symbols. Why use symbols? What do they do?

Symbols were used in systems of healing long before Usui. To Usui, symbols in Reiki do not have magical powers. Symbols are used to dial, metaphorically speaking, particular frequencies or groups of frequencies in the Reiki bandwidth.

Usui taught his Reiki II students three symbols. One symbol is for Power, one is for Mental/Emotional healing, and one is for Distant healing. The symbols for power and Mental/Emotional healing have names in Japanese, although the shape of those symbols does not relate to their names.

The symbol for Power increases the power of basic Reiki. The symbol for Mental/Emotional healing does what its name says. The Distant Reiki symbol sends Reiki energy across distance – across a room, across a state, across the planet. This third capability of Reiki can only be described by Quantum physics.

The symbols are considered sacred. Traditionally they are kept private, out of respect. I am not including a picture of these symbols (though you can find them on the Internet) out of respect for the tradition that withholds them from students until they are actually attuned to the ability to use them. If you look them up, simply seeing them will not give you the ability to practice Reiki.

Students gain the ability from a Reiki Master who was attuned by another Master and so on up the line to Usui.

From my Western point of view, it seems to me that symbols facilitate learning. The symbols assist perceptive sensitivity by giving a visual key to the vibration that is being felt, sometimes almost imperceptibly, because the Reiki vibrations can be nearly undetectable to some beginning students. I believe when the student memorizes a symbol, he or she is at the same time feeling very subtly the vibration associated with it. Every time the student names, visualizes or draws a symbol, intending to heal in a particular way, Reiki energy responds accordingly. As time goes by, any Reiki student's ability to perceive the symbols' vibrations can increase and cross the threshold into conscious awareness. Meanwhile, the student can practice effectively anyway.

A very clear explanation of what is happening physically when one learns to use symbols can be found in an article by William Lee Rand, Usui Reiki Symbols on his ICRT website, *https://www. reiki.org/reikinews/usuisym.html.*

Experiencing Reiki

It is important to realize that everyone experiences Reiki in his or her own way. We can learn a lot from sharing experiences, yet the biggest lesson is, to accept it as it shows up, without expecting your awareness of the energy to be the same as anyone else's.

When you take a Reiki class, remember the energy is new to you. Give yourself a chance to get acquainted with it. Practice may improve your awareness of the energy. My Reiki I experience was a class of one – me. I caution against learning in such a tiny class because you lose the richness of experience that is possible when several or more students are learning together, practicing on each other, and sharing their experiences with each other.

Classes usually offer a number of opportunities to experience Reiki and to talk about your experiences. The conversation helps you identify what you are feeling. From that point on, you can grow in ability to perceive the energy. (Note section on Byosen, later.) Usui expected that all students could develop ability to understand what the feelings they experience are indicating about the person being treated.

Everyday Practice

If you use Reiki daily, your understanding of what Reiki can do will grow. You are likely to see new uses for it, and you'll also notice unexpected changes for the good in your own health and personality.

Beware of limiting your practice on yourself to body parts that feel uncomfortable. Reiki does much more for you than healing discomfort. At first, you are exercising your ability and increasing your awareness. It helps to hold a positive attitude. Say to yourself, "I want to feel Reiki more," instead of, "I can't feel Reiki as much as I want to."

When I understood how important my attitude was, I finally took the advice I just gave you. I began *giving everything* Reiki. I had heard of people giving their car Reiki when it wouldn't start, for instance, but I didn't try that. I gave Reiki to food, drinks, vitamins, my bed (intending sound sleep), books I needed to read (intending to increase my concentration and allow freedom in thinking), piles of papers I needed to sort for taxes, and the like.

There is a common practice called *imbuing* by which one intends to soak an object or process in Reiki in order to change it beneficially, or make it a carrier of Reiki energy. An example of this will be provided in Chapter 8.

My intent when I gave Reiki to things or situations was to change myself, my own energy. My mind becomes clearer and I can organize things or ideas more quickly when I ask Reiki to flow. The result for me was that practice quickly increased my awareness of Reiki.

Early Reiki Masters, especially Usui and Dr. Hayashi, were more interested in becoming aware of the energy in people they treated than in being aware of energy in themselves.

Your teacher will have exercises in class that help you begin to notice the energy. Some exercises help you notice Reiki in yourself. Some help you notice disturbance in other people. After you take a class, it will be helpful to find other exercises to expand your sensitivity to other people. I suggest two small books, The Original Reiki Handbook of Dr. Mikao Usui (ISBN: 9780914955573, Lotus Press 1999), and The Hayashi Reiki Manual (ISBN 978-0914955757 Lotus Press 2003), neither one contains the entire original Master's manual of Usui or Dr. Hayashi. Instead, only the practical parts are translated. Copious photo illustrations are added which make following along much easier. (By the way, referring to the title above, Usui was not a medical doctor. Some people use the term *Dr.* for him, I believe as an honorific.)

If you take Reiki to support yourself, or a loved one with a particular health challenge, you may find helpful advice in either of these books. Meanwhile, treating parts known to be affected works well. Using Mrs. Takata's system of hand positions for a complete body treatment is also effective, especially when some organs may not be consciously painful, even though they are actually involved in the condition being treated.

Beneficial personality changes can result for anybody, usually over a period of time, as the stories provided by Chellie Kammermeyer attest. My experience with Jennifer McLean's work led me to notice, and then explain in Chapter 2, that the very deep rest achieved during a Reiki session RELEASES strongly repressed emotional memories. In my experience as a Reiki practitioner, I also receive Reiki energy while I am giving it, so I experience benefits from giving it too.

Reiki-share

In most areas of the country you'll be able to find a Reiki-share. A Reiki-share is a gathering of practitioners who share Reiki with each other and often discuss their experiences. A Reiki-share is a valuable learning venue during your early days of practice. It is also always wonderful to be a recipient of Reiki from another practitioner, so the Reiki-share benefits practitioners at all levels of experience. The experience of receiving is always deeply refreshing.

Byosen

The early Japanese Masters valued sensitivity highly. As I've said, Usui taught students to pay careful attention to the feelings in their hands.

When energy is moving normally in the body, it is not usually noticed. Usui believed that ailments, including those stemming from a mental or emotional cause, are detectable by practitioners because the body's energy patterns become disturbed. The disturbances were called *Byosen*. Byosen is a two-word phrase, *byo* and *sen*, that literally mean *sick* and *accumulation*. In Reiki, the word Byosen refers to energetic disturbances that the practitioner can feel by passing hands over each client's body.

Some people feel energetic disturbances in other people as heat or a tingle or even pain, and these differences were early on believed to indicate intensity of the physical disturbance. Awareness can grow as the student exercises Reiki. Usui used students' level of awareness as a guideline for readiness to be attuned to the next highest level. Awareness can grow even beyond the Master level.

There is another strong reason to develop sensitivity to Byosen. A sensitive practitioner can often notice areas where the body is calling for treatment, even though those spots had not registered as painful to the client. The Byosen scan alerts the practitioner, who is not usually medically trained, to areas of the body that may not be painful but nevertheless need attention.

Byosen was originally expected to provide adequate diagnoses. Such diagnoses were considered acceptable because Byosen was seen as an empirical practice, in that the awareness of Byosen was believed to be sensory evidence of the client's condition. In the West, we want more. We want a thorough medical examination and diagnosis using the techniques and language we have grown to trust.

There are people today, however, who ask Reiki practitioners "what they got" from their scan of the client's body. Some practitioners can answer because they have an unusual ability to diagnose intuitively, enough to call a "gift." Attunement creates ability to share Reiki, but attunement does not give *unusual* ability. As a practitioner, I never claim to diagnose. I do not have the abilities involved in intuitive diagnosis. I personally leave diagnosis to the medical profession, as we know it in the West. On the other hand – I am delighted to apply Reiki in cases where diagnosis has been sought, but not found, because I have found that relief can often be had by using Reiki in those cases.

There is no end to learning Reiki

Usui himself believed that there is no limit to the quality and effectiveness of the Reiki energy available in the universe. This meant to him that practitioners could always improve their transmittal of the Reiki energy. Usui's impulse to re-attune his students multiple times seems consistent with this belief. William Lee Rand has been attuned many times from different teachers, and attributes his ability and insight to that fact.

Ultimately, there can be no end to new uses of Reiki as long as the universe expands and we human beings continue to adapt to its expansion.

The Reiki bandwidth is what it is. It does what it does whether the patient believes in it or not, the way electricity lights up a light bulb whether we believe in electricity or not. The practitioner does not control what Reiki does, although the symbols introduce nuances that practitioners can select to emphasize certain qualities, such as healing mental or emotional distress, or healing at a distance.

There is a caveat to this mechanistic view of the action of Reiki: Reiki works because the practitioner intends for it to flow, *and* the recipient *consents* to receive it. It seems that sometimes the recipient unconsciously refuses to receive it. Practitioners usually say that Reiki respects human freedom.

Chapter 8

Extensions and Applications

In Chapter 5, I shared examples of the effects of Reiki when practiced long-term. Long-term beneficial results of many kinds can occur even if your primary intention is simply physical comfort. When you use Reiki, new ideas, ideas that harmonize with your deepest purposes, will certainly appear and enhance your life.

Here I offer reports of several people who did their own thing with Reiki, expecting that you, too, can make a difference in your own place, way and time.

A Handful of Applications

Besides self-care, Reiki is useful in circumstances you might not think of without reading examples. (This, by the way, is a function of Reiki News Magazine. While it is all good news, not fear-filled commentaries on current events, additionally, Reiki News Magazine gives you a view of possibilities you might have never considered.)

Writes Carra, a friend:

Propelled by the passion for health and self-care that had led me into nursing, in the 1990s I learned a variety of non-standard healing modalities, including Reiki. A friend offered the classes, so taking them seemed natural. We students had a practice group at a local hospital, and I volunteered with another friend at a local animal shelter. The woman supervisor shared that the animals always seemed to know when we were coming, and were almost always at their most settled after our visit. The cats especially would respond, coming to the front of their enclosures to be as close as possible to the energy.

Time spent with the animals was enjoyable and satisfying, but I wondered why Reiki had shown up in my life. Four years later, I found out.

My mother was dying from bone cancer then. She was in her 80s, a long life that had been challenging in many ways. Pain from her cancer was well controlled by medication, but pain in her feet persisted. The problem with her feet had predated her cancer by many years and caused severe pain when she walked. During my prior visit, the pain had been so severe that she could not allow covers over her feet, and was extremely guarded lest someone accidentally touch them.

I offered to give her Reiki. After initial hesitation she accepted, though she made me promise not to touch her feet. I sat at the foot of her bed, making no physical contact, but beaming *Reiki using my eyes focused on some part of her body or feet. She told me almost immediately that she could feel something, and asked if I were touching her feet. I reassured her, and suggested that the two of us play a game. (I invented the game on the spot.)*

I told her I would give Reiki without touching her. Her part in the game would be to tell me where she felt it.

My intention was to help her relax, because she seemed so anxious, and worried that I would do too much. We agreed to stop whenever she felt she was done.

We both felt the flow of energy. I saw in my mind's eye the energy move up her body and she told me where she felt it move. Then simultaneously we said, "Done."

I looked at her feet, and to my surprise in my mind's eye saw toes horribly bent backwards into the arch, the small toe almost back to the heel. Without a doubt, those deformities would be consistent with a bound foot, a custom in China generations ago. Could her pain stem from a past life in China, I wondered. My speculation was unimportant, compared to my shock at what happened next.

My mother asked me if I would rub her feet.

I gently massaged each foot, as one would rub a newborn baby. A few days later, she peacefully left her body.

Can you imagine how helpful it might be to loved-ones, if you learn Reiki? Or if hospice nurses were all equipped to share Reiki? Or if Reiki practitioners joined hospice teams? Do you realize that this woman with pain in her feet could have been helped years before her death? Her daughter's experience can suggest to us that there are so many possible applications of Reiki that I can't write them all in this book.

This story illustrates how Reiki can suddenly show up at an unexpected time in life. It comes into your mind, it comes as an idea, and you have to choose to follow through with it, or not. If you choose to apply it, you'll discover new ways to enhance your life and that of other people as well.

Drum-roll, please!

An early student of the ICRT system (International Center for Reiki Training, *www.reiki.org*), named Michael Arthur Baird, developed a quite different application. Michael had been a professional drummer before he studied under William Lee Rand (more on Rand in Chapter 9). Michael became a Reiki Master and in 1999 incorporated drumming into his Reiki practice. Thus he established a new treatment modality. I'm classifying this as an *application* because he uses Reiki along with drumming. Reiki is not different, the drum is simply imbued with Reiki; or else Reiki is used in a standard way, alternating with or accompanied by drumming. Of course, Michael calls his technique Reiki Drumming. Michael also developed a manual to pass on his technique for using Reiki with a drum for healing.

Michael now teaches Reiki and also his method of Reiki practice with a drum. He uses a frame drum, in several ways. Not all clients want to include hearing a drum during their Reiki session, so he recommends the use of noise-reducing headphones for the ear-sensitive folk who want to try this modality. For me, the louder the better, and it has been very enriching experience every time I've had it done for me. Along with the Reiki bandwidth, one experiences vibrations of the drum which themselves elicit natural responses in the human body. The drum vibrations can break a dysfunctional cycle set up by the mind, so the drum in itself can create a break in tension similar to the break that hand-applied Reiki does. The power of drumming has been an important factor in human experience for eons.

For some clients, memories show up that spin out and release buried emotions. For me, memories sometimes show up as though they were of past lives. Whether we really have past lives or not, the thoughts at least bring to consciousness real present conflicts that have sunk into the unconscious. One result for me is a helpful energetic release. My experience has shown that the effect of the drum combined with Reiki can be profound.

If this interests you, ask the practitioner you are seeing whether he or she knows of it. Not every practitioner knows about Reiki drumming. Not to worry if drumming sounds unpleasant to you. Even if it is available you are free to choose not to use it.

Michael shares a website *http://reikiclasses.com* and Reiki practice with his wife Laurelle Gaia at Peace Place Healing Center in Sedona, AZ.

Sabine's Reiki scarves

(You heard from Sabine when she told her story in Chapter 5 about using Reiki for healing cats in a veterinarian's clinic.)

The Reiki scarves are a method I teach as an expansion for my Reiki II students, and this is how it developed:

Three of my loved ones were seriously to terminally ill at the same time, all of them savoring Reiki treatments, all of them benefiting from Reiki. I also had my own normal life and my work ... and two of them lived a two hours' drive away from me... so I just needed an idea, and it came. I received the idea of how to infuse objects with Reiki in a way that they served as a kind of reservoir.

I am a skeptical person. We all know – faith can move mountains (which is a good thing). One of my ill loved ones, however, was my cat (you already met him). You can tell a cat any story you like, he will certainly not be very impressed by it, let alone make a belief out of it. Placebo-stories just don't work with animals. That's not to say anything negative about placebo-stories – quite the contrary, in my opinion they are the most elegant (and scientifically proven most effective) way of healing imaginable! If you are talented at telling placebo-stories… just forget about any other healing modality, or use it to make every other healing so much more powerful!

I made a Reiki cushion *and put it in one of his baskets. He went to that basket just like he came on my lap when he* asked *for Reiki. If you don't have a pet, it is hard to describe, may it suffice to say that you can see or feel that there is a difference, whether they come for Reiki or for being petted. And especially the way they get up, when they feel they had enough Reiki for now, is unique. He used that basket like a service station to get* filled *with Reiki. He never again used it to take a normal nap. I could also see that when he left the basket his limping had improved. That was proof for me that it worked and was more than just imagination.*

Starting from this prototype, things developed naturally. I found materials that worked better than others, in which Reiki would stick *longer and would be released more smoothly, I found out that there is a much easier and faster way than to quilt the symbols into the cushion or blanket. And I also learned from my cat that these things need their own kind of* energy-washing, *or he would not use it anymore after a while.*

You can imagine how happy and grateful I was, and still am, for being given such a gift.

When I finally felt my normal winter-cold approaching with a sore throat and hoarseness (which for decades had always run its same course of at least 10 days) – I gave myself a Reiki scarf (in addition to my normal mega dose vitamin regimen, which on its own, however, had never had such an impressive effect). Believe it or not – within a day or two the sore throat was gone and none of the other usual symptoms developed. Over the years this happened many times. And each and every time I could stop the cold in its tracks - if I don't wait too long. But even then it helps to let the cold run a much milder course.

So, why am I sharing this?

First, to give you another example, that there are countless possibilities for Reiki applications.

Second, to show you that there are even ways to give Reiki with negligible expenditure of time, that run on (a kind of programmable) auto-pilot, and leave your hands and head free for whatever needs to be done. Of course having an hour of Reiki, relaxed, with closed eyes and soft music in the background is marvelous … but …

can I do this whenever I think this would make me feel well? Usually I can't, and with this method it means I do not have to go without or with just a little Reiki.

And, most importantly, to encourage you to experiment – you only need love as your foundation, and you will find something wonderful.

I am sorry that I cannot teach you the method here, but if you are interested to learn it, and you are already attuned to Reiki II or III, please feel free to contact me (See Contacts page at the end of this book).

Honest Talk about Self-care

Self-care using Reiki was not Usui's idea. Not that he opposed it, he just didn't talk or write about it, as far as we know. The first important person we know to recommend self-care was Mrs. Takata. Self-care is not an application as I'm using that term here, but self-care is a topic itself and deserves attention.

Face the fact that our national culture does not value rest. In some national cultures, vacations are important. In ours, working hard and long gets more credit. Multitasking is a norm, even though it can be counter-productive. Changing careers is a norm, changing employers is a norm. Divorce is normal; single-parent homes are normal.

All of these norms raise our everyday stress level way beyond tolerable. The negative impact of stress on our health has made news in recent years, but culturally we have not taken notice. You'll be swimming upstream if you take Reiki seriously. You'll need to give yourself credit, as well as allowing yourself Reiki.

If you are a caregiver, you deserve more appreciation than you get. You also deserve as much Reiki as you give, not because giving Reiki *takes something OUT of you* – that doesn't happen, you ALWAYS get, while you give. It's the stress of everything ELSE that you do that really calls for Reiki-relief. You stuff a lot of that stress into apparent oblivion that could easily change energetic form into resentment, discouragement or depression. You really WANT to be a cheerful giver and find fulfillment in giving. You want to become a fulfilled human being in many other aspects of life, too. Fulfillment – or at least satisfaction – CAN occur during caretaking if you also take care of yourself.

Whenever you give yourself Reiki, be careful to notice changes, even very slight ones, consciously. Focus on each change as it happens. Focus on feeling better than you did before doing Reiki, rather than complaining if some pain or stiffness remains. Attention to the new condition breaks the centrality of pain that sets up and increases our perception of pain so easily.

Meanwhile, realize that many conditions did not form overnight, but actually result from pre-existing tensions. Many of us have had a *One last straw* experience, which can bring a pre-formed set of symptoms to the forefront. Be kind to yourself. Give yourself time. Remember that many medications caution that they could take weeks to begin to resolve your symptoms.

Please be assured, Reiki is not addictive. No matter how much you enjoy getting it or giving it, you never come to a day when your feelings are in charge. Reiki does not call to you through feelings or emotions, not even for soothing. You have to

DECIDE to use Reiki. You may say, "I don't have an urge," to use Reiki – on myself, or on anybody else – but that is not an appropriate excuse. Reiki requires that you CHOOSE to use it, and then *allow* it to have whatever effect it has on you.

This is important to realize, because it is so easy to overlook using Reiki, especially on yourself. For many of us it is easier to think of the needs of other people than it is to think of our own. I suspect that an important driving force in any of us is love – and our love for certain other people is much stronger than our love for ourselves.

Applying Reiki to yourself, for your own good, has to be done by routine, on a schedule – first, during your snooze alarm nap, then Reiki your morning snack. Decide routine times to fit Reiki into your day – during an afternoon pick-me-up, or a bedtime routine. The more times you allow Reiki to flow for you by plan, the more using it will come to mind spontaneously.

Whether you ask Reiki to flow on your own behalf or to someone else, listen to your character as well as your ideals. Elsewhere I have mentioned that

I personally am impatient. For me, that means to start with whatever treatment methods are easily available, already tried and true, including meds.

Do not martyr yourself or your loved ones by insisting on proceeding only using your ideal method. (Of course I hope that Reiki is your ideal method.) Use what is already being recommended medically, and add Reiki to that. Let results speak for themselves, and allow changes to come in their own time.

Intent

Another point about using Reiki is the need to use *intent*. Just intend that Reiki flow – to someone, or a group of people, or a thing. You are choosing a direction of the flow. You could include *for the good*, *for their highest good* or some other similar phrase. Reiki never causes harm, however, so saying *for (highest) good* is redundant, as far as Reiki is concerned.

It seems to me that *intending* is not simply a passive array of energies in your brain. It is clear to me that many intentions arrange patterns of nerve response ordinarily bringing about action. We do not usually notice this very subtle shift of energy. It came to my attention when I began to experiment with what is called *animal communication*. Sitting with my young cat on my lap, I want him to move so I can write more comfortably. To win cooperation, I say softly, "Let's go downstairs to take a nap." I feel my own muscles tense, preparing to stand up. After a moment, Kitten's head rises from his curled rest, and his eyes widen. I speak softly again, and alertness springs up in his body. "Let's go!" I say a third time. He hops down, and heads for the stairs.

As we consciously streamline our work to make it easier to do our tasks, we unconsciously pre-set patterns of behavior as well. Innocent enough is our *morning routine*. We rise easily or grumpily, as usual; then shower, or not, as usual. We dress and make coffee or tea and maybe a bite of breakfast. The routine is a habit pattern we work out or fall into, and it feels strange if some part of that routine is broken.

Sometimes intent comes naturally and unnoticed. For instance, when a practitioner's energy is being tested for scientific measurement the intent is clear and simple: it is to *do Reiki*. When we ask Reiki to flow to another person, we are more likely to use intent consciously. At least, we *intend to help* that person. So the flow of energy is unimpeded by doubt and confusion. When we try to apply Reiki to ourselves, we can easily notice when our intent is confused, by thoughts like, "Will this really work for me?" and "I don't have time for this."

Return to the topic, More "more"

I believe *intentional* self-care is a stage in experience. *Stage* means there is a goal, or at least a vision we pursue. Whether we have a goal or not, and no matter what our goal might be, if we are using Reiki along our way, we'll become more humane than we are now. We can become kinder to each other than we are now. I expect the day will come when we are gentler even to our own Self.

I believe we can live rational lives, guided by our heart for humanity – for our advancement socially, personally, economically. I believe we can create wise choices to achieve a sustainable approach to natural resources that are so lavish on our planet. Reiki can heal our minds, help us regulate our emotions, and yield to us the kind of life we all want.

I believe consistent use of Reiki for friends and family will build the personal confidence in each of us that we can actually accomplish goals we have only dreamed of. I believe the use of Reiki will motivate us to create the energetic structure within each of us that supports wisdom, peace and freedom for all of us. We can do this, and using Reiki it'll be easy.

There really are solutions to our problems. When we relax, the habit of allowing our lives to be run by reactive emotional charges vanishes. We'll find solutions more easily when we release the dysfunctional beliefs and emotional repressions that naturally stem from childhood. We'll be able to look at ourselves honestly, and begin to notice patterns of behavior that stand in the way of seeing what isn't working for us.

Cutthroat competition can be more harmful than helpful. We can play well with others when we play well with our own Self. We can reach our goals. Reiki, universal energy that heals, is everywhere, and useable by nearly everyone. Meditation works easily, if you start by meditating your body.

Chapter 9

Expanding Our Vision

We've reached the point in this book to announce conclusions. Whatever your original purpose for practicing Reiki could be – physical comfort during illness or stress-reduction in the midst of challenges – you'll find a yield of emotional and mental satisfaction beyond your wildest imagination. I did, so I believe that you can, too.

Beyond satisfying your own needs, practice of Reiki molds you into a person whose very being improves the quality of life for people around you. Your healed and organized energy contributes to positive creative forces on this planet. You become a center radiating good energy. That is your nature.

Every improvement you make in your own life has a good effect on everyone around you. As your energy improves and increases, it inevitably expands outward. What you do for yourself will make a contribution towards the good of humanity. Whatever you do with your improved energy will make its mark improving our planet.

Reiki for transformation

Have you noticed we are living in a stressful, chaotic landscape? Humanity is going through a major change. Attitudes we thought had been outgrown have come to the forefront again: name-calling, hasty generalization, blaming, bullying and the like. These behaviors seem almost genteel, in comparison to physical violence, but the manner in which they are being used seems to me to be hate infused. We see a rising tide of violence at home and worldwide. We are challenged to develop new ways to deal with these chronic conditions.

I want physical healing for all of you, I want stress-free living for all of you – but this book is written to be more than a how-to manual to achieve those ends. I want you all to find the emotional stability and mental clarity that have come to me as a result of using Reiki.

Yes, I have worked intentionally to reach those ends, but I know anyone can do what I have done, and I see how much the qualities of emotional stability and mental clarity are needed on our planet today. I certainly don't mean to promise that Reiki is the highest, or only, answer to living a productive, satisfying, eco-friendly life. But Reiki can do so much.

Despite our social challenges, we now have an OPPORTUNITY to act on our awareness of our interdependence as human beings. Social media provides a new channel of significant fuel into our lives. We have worldwide instant communication. We have deeper and broader access to each other than we have ever had. An amazing depth, breadth and searchability of data now available can allow extensive knowledge of planetary resources. At the same time, the multiplicity of resources threatens to overwhelm us.

We have an opportunity to assess our planetary resources and manage them carefully for the good of all. We have begun to choose to use sustainable resources of energy to sustain our level of civilization. We are able to investigate the genetic structures of individuals and create new technologies for medical intervention. Now we can perform relatively complicated surgeries by using comparatively tiny incisions. We can give catastrophically injured people – and pets – bionic limbs. We are on the brink of a new medicine, the practice of regeneration – of cartilage, for instance – which in itself will transform ageing as we have known it.

I have been showing you how recent science has been able to study functions of human energy fields. We can now confirm that these human-generated fields can be used to support and sometimes replace surgery or chemical medicine. I believe it is no accident that Reiki came into view early in the 1900s, just as the change from power generated by material resources to nuclear power occurred. Our knowledge of the universe expanded in all directions at once and revealed to us new capabilities.

In this age of rapid change, human beings are changing too. We are doing more than expanding and upgrading social and technological possibilities for human life on this planet. Our very physical being, possibly the DNA of humanity and certainly its expressions, are changing. This has always been the case (in biology we call these changes *mutations*) but we have only recently begun to see this scientifically.

Reiki and human potential

We all make choices. The common remark, "Oh, people never change," only verbalizes a depressed attitude. People *can* and *do* change. Some changes seem to happen to us. Sometimes, change eludes us because we are simply reacting to circumstances. We can *choose* change, though. We can change when we decide to.

Reiki presents a new wrinkle for human potential. In the 1960s, the idea that human beings might have untapped abilities was expanded and developed in psychology and education, and called The Human Potential Movement. The movement was roundly criticized. At the same time, stories in The Magazine of Fantasy and Science Fiction explored human capabilities, such as telepathy, that were considered to be only imaginary. Experiments in parapsychology at Duke University attempted to establish that telepathy could be real. Could it be that these hopeful dreams persisted and mutated into present-day super-heroes in comic books and movies? Could it be true that some of those dreams were intuitions of yet-untapped possibilities?

Suspicious people have viewed Reiki as an exotic extrasensory phenomenon. If that were true, then it's no wonder that any result attributed to Reiki would be suspect; results would probably be merely coincidental. Now that Reiki is found to be measurable, and studying Reiki and its results can be done within the scientific framework, we can see a new future for human potential.

Despite the backlash in the sixties against the possibility of substantial human development, the thinking lives on that humankind does have untapped possibilities and can change in unexpected ways that could benefit us enormously. Reiki provides one of those possibilities.

War might once have been seen helpful, to "decrease the surplus population", as Dickens' Scrooge hoped darkly, but now its effects are global. War is no longer a sustainable solution to relationship problems. There are too many negative consequences for the human race and for the planet. We can choose to shift our battles inside, to our individual selves. We can release the *battle* imagery and simply declare INTENT, knowing that intent is the truly effective agent to marshal our energy. We can move toward cooperative behavior. We can improve our relationship to this planet that sustains us. Reiki can help us to accomplish all these changes in behavior.

The Sweep of History

Reiki showed up on its own, so to speak. No one sat down to invent it, yet it – or something similar – showed up to at least four separate participants, who all lived in Japan and lived within a fairly brief time-period early in the twentieth century. Isn't this a strange coincidence? Did something happen? I'm just asking.

As time has gone by, Reiki has been practiced in various styles, with various techniques. Treatments have been given in several ways, students have been taught several different systems, and initiation (practical access to Reiki energy, *attunement*, or *placement* and *ignition*) has been given in several ways. Yet Reiki is effective in all these variations.

Let's look at a wave of change

Into the mix of Usui-lineage Reiki teachers came William Lee Rand in 1989. Hailing from Southfield, a suburb of Detroit, Michigan, he studied Reiki in 1989 in the United States with two different Reiki Masters. He opened his own business in June that year. He studied both the Usui/Takata tradition, and an innovative application of Reiki created by Arthur Robertson. Robertson's system had added symbols from Tibet and a technique called Violet Breath. Notice, however, that Robertson began his creative work by being attuned in the Usui tradition.

Rand combined the Usui/Takata tradition with Robertson's Tibetan elements into a system of his own, and taught this from 1989 till 2014. I was introduced to Reiki I by an Usui-teacher, and went on to Reiki I and II together (twice), with two different Usui-based masters. I took Rand's Master class in 2007, and was attuned as Reiki Master in Rand's system, including Tibetan symbols and Violet Breath.

Rand created the International Center for Reiki Training, wrote manuals for Reiki I and II as well as Master training, and taught thousands of students around the world. Through the ICRT he established accreditation for teachers of Reiki in his own system. He created numerous CDs as aids in teaching and for general interest.

He wanted to be as thorough, as precise as possible, in passing on the traditions of Reiki. His interest in the origins of Reiki took him to Japan to research Reiki's early history, which resulted in his book, An Evidence Based History of Reiki (ISBN-13: 9781886785410, published by International Center for Reiki Training, 2014). He re-introduced Usui's original Master symbol, as well as an attunement for it, and created a one-day event he called ART (Advanced Reiki Training). His ART class teaches how crystals can be used in healing with Reiki, including a Reiki Grid that employs crystals to send Reiki continuously. He also includes the concept and practice of *aura clearing*.

Rand's point of view is expansive; he encourages his students to accept all applications and extensions of Reiki. *The proof is in the pudding* – extensions or applications are effective and, in my experience as well as the thousands of ICRT practitioners, do not cause harm.

The following paragraphs describe a development in ICRT that could be seen as not appropriately called Reiki. William Lee Rand himself describes the energy as similar, but different, and felt guided to trademark the name.

Karuna Reiki

Not long after starting his business, Rand experienced an influx of students who showed him symbols he had not seen before and asked whether he knew them. He kept the symbols, with whatever he heard about them. Another wave of students appeared, people who had heard of other teachers teaching unfamiliar symbols. This wave wanted to know if Rand was going to teach them. Rand declined and sent those students back to the people who were teaching them. There was no escape however. The students returned, asking Rand to investigate those symbols and teach them himself.

The process of studying, testing and creating a new class for teaching these new symbols took two years, between 1993 and 1995. The result was a system eventually called Karuna Reiki. Rand felt guided to trademark the name. Karuna (a word meaning *care* in Sanskrit) Reiki has eight symbols that tune to wavelengths that function in areas we might call *depth psychology*. Karuna Reiki assists in healing unconscious or deeply repressed areas of the human mind and emotions, and assists many other wonderful biofield energetic changes.

Rand says carefully, "The reason I chose to use the term Reiki for Karuna Reiki is that Karuna healing energy is a Reiki-like energy in that it is life force energy that is guided by the higher power." (From website article by William Lee Rand, Karuna Reiki® Questions and Answers, *https://www.reiki.org/reikinews/rn970103.html*. See the answer to the fourth question, "Why do you use the term Reiki ...?")

Rand requires that one be attuned to Usui Master level before studying Karuna Reiki.

Holy Fire Reiki

Following the formation of Karuna Reiki in 1995-6, another creative energy wave hit Rand in 2014. He called it Holy Fire Reiki. During a session with Janice Jones, a spiritual advisor he had met with for 19 years, Rand became "aware of a healing energy that was more refined and contained a higher level of consciousness than anything I had previously experienced... The energy around this experience was so clear and powerful that I trusted what I was told," he wrote (See *https://www.reiki.org/FAQ/HistoryOfReiki.html*, segment entitled Holy Fire Reiki, next to last paragraph in the article).

The Tibetan elements of Rand's Reiki system were taken out of use, while the Usui symbols were retained. The process by which access to Reiki is passed on became much simpler. In attunements (traditional language), Holy Fire Reiki eliminates direct intervention by the teaching Master. In Holy Fire Reiki the teaching Master invites the students to enter a meditative state, and provides simple instructions to assist them. The state is not controlled by the guiding paragraphs, however, so the guidance is not canned nor is it magic. Any similar wordings work. Each student allows him/herself to enter a meditative state, and in that state receives the changes necessary to transmit Reiki. In effect, Holy Fire students seem to be doing what Usui himself did when he first received Reiki.

Holy Fire language uses the word *placement* for attunement during both Reiki I and Reiki II, and uses the term *ignition* for attuning to Master's level and to Holy Fire Karuna Reiki. This change in language was an insight Rand attained during his receipt of the Holy Fire system. He emphasizes that during the reception of the ability to do Holy Fire Reiki, no ritual is involved, so no individual person's energy field is controlling the change.

Rand teaches that since the Reiki energy alone is acting upon each recipient, the *placement* received is free of limitation by any human and thus is stronger and purer than Reiki can be if it depends on a human intermediary to transmit the ability.

Rand's students have amazing experiences during the meditations that pass Holy Fire on to them. Those who received the Master's attunement in his earlier system (including me) now report that Holy Fire Reiki works better on their clients.

Holy Fire Reiki was upgraded to Holy Fire II in 2016. Rand writes about that change in a blog, Holy Fire II Upgrade "The nature of Holy Fire energy is that it is continually evolving and developing. This takes place within each student after the training. In addition, as our Holy Fire Reiki energy develops, we become ready for major upgrades that are transmitted during a Holy Fire class." I personally attest to experiencing these changes. In my mind, these changes are consistent with Usui's own belief that our practice of Reiki energy is infinitely perfectible.

During 2018, the Holy Fire energy upgraded again to Holy Fire III. Rand introduced it to his Licensed teachers and several Master's classes, late in the year, and to his Holy Fire II students in January, 2019.

WE are making history

This has always been true. Human beings have always expanded the universe by their creativity. The history we make now has opened many new possibilities. We are making history in a different way than people have before. Until now, action-reaction has been the name of our game. If you fight me, I'll fight you back.

We are beginning to be more aware of our freedom, and increasing in our ability to exercise free choice. We are more aware of our freedom to claim who we really are.

I believe these changes are evolutionary, in a positive sense. God, Creator, is at work. I believe our changes are directional, and for the better. When we learn Reiki and practice it, we are changing ourselves for the better. When we personally change for the better, our new energy affects both people and the environment positively. We change everyone we touch with Reiki for the better. When we use Reiki, we are joining in the positive evolutionary flow of energy the planet is exhibiting now.

Please note: whichever version of Reiki you find, whichever choice of Reiki is available to you, whichever variation of Reiki you practice, in any of them you are contributing to good, wellness, and wholeness in this planet.

Have you ever heard about "the 10%"?

Critical Mass

The idea of *critical mass* is best known from nuclear physics. A critical mass in nuclear physics is the smallest amount of material that can initiate a sustained chain-reaction. The idea of critical mass was adopted and adapted by studies of social dynamics. A critical mass in a social system is the number or percentage of individuals required to propagate a social innovation.

100th Monkey Effect

A well-known example of social critical mass is called the *100th monkey effect*. Scientists discovered this by accident in 1952 when studying Japanese Macaca monkeys on the island of Koshima. Scientists fed the monkeys by dropping sweet potatoes on the sand. The monkeys liked the taste of the sweet potatoes, but not the taste of the sand that stuck to them. An 18-month old female washed her potatoes in a stream, and taught her mother the trick. It seemed that sweet potatoes free of sand were preferable. That monkey's playmates learned the trick too, and taught their mothers.

Between 1952 and 1958, all the young monkeys learned to wash their sweet potatoes, and so did all their mothers. None of the other monkeys changed their behavior.

Suddenly in the fall of 1958, ALL of the monkeys began washing their sweet potatoes. Scientists created the conjecture that there had been a particular point at which one more monkey washing somehow created the breakthrough. Although they had no real count, it seemed accurate to say, 99 monkeys were not enough monkeys to change the behavior of the remainder, but the 100th provided the energy needed to initiate the change. (My "robust sense of reality" – referring to Bertrand Russell's famous quote - is kicking up a bit, but this theory caught interest and the thinking spread.)

The scientists were startled to discover that after this breakthrough point, monkeys on other islands began to wash their potatoes. When the new behavior began on other islands, it began with only a few monkeys. The process of spreading to other monkeys was the same as on Koshima. Older monkeys never began the process of washing their potatoes and they joined the washing group only after the critical mass was reached. Younger monkeys and their mothers changed, and thereby started the process.

Does this ring a bell to you? Sounds like ...

Furthermore, the process of change here looks very much like the process of entrainment, described in Chapter 6.

The 10%

In 2011 scientists at the Rensselaer Polytechnic Institute using computer analysis found that when 10% of a population hold a firm belief, it becomes a majority belief. **Read that sentence again – If 10% of a population changes, the change can and will continue.** Sounds like 10% of a population functions as a critical mass.

This finding contradicts our habitual understanding of *majority*, and our practice of democracy. As a democracy, we presume that "the majority rules". We define a *majority* as more than 50%. There is some comfort in expecting it would take half our population to rule us. Could only 10% of us succeed in ruling our opinions?

How many in this nation are now involved in the sudden shift in weight of opinion since 2016, from conventional politeness, global thinking, and the rule of law, to name-calling, white supremacy, and the rule of personal fire-power? Is our country's central strength faltering because most of us hold opinions very loosely? You might say most of us are wishy-washy.

In self-defense, I want to say that I have held opinions quietly instead of forthrightly. There is a reason to speak quietly. I believe that no claim is true simply because it is shouted. How often have you noticed people shouting their beliefs, as if screaming emphatically would make their beliefs true?

Plato held that "To know the Good is to DO the Good." Maybe life is not that simple. Maybe truth has less power than Plato expected.

The Rensselaer study suggests that Truth does not have force in itself. In a social setting, force (might) can dominate irrespective of empirical proof. *Truth* that is found by intuitive means may well be completely true, but the parameters for coming to social agreement on intuitive truths have not been well established. The bottom line we must take into account is, that **Truth can lose its force when its voice is drowned out by a mere 10%.**

"Might Makes Right"

When I studied Plato in college, I thrilled to the scene in The Republic where Thrasymachus argues, "might makes right," and Socrates is depicted convincingly arguing Mr. T's claim is invalid. I believed then in Truth with a capital T. Truth that would everywhere and always be true. I eventually learned that could not be demonstrated to be the case. The history of Western philosophy and the history of Western science have both shown the conditionality of truth. Truth arises in each observer but observing itself alters each observation.

It is not appropriate, as some people now espouse, to say that there are *alternative truths*. There is truth and there is error and there are opinions. There are *alternative universes* and two systems of physics (Quantum and Newtonian), but only ONE truth – even if we have not formulated a Unified Field Theory to substantiate our claim, the human goal IS One Truth, Unified Truth.

Any truth is a stable component in a configuration of truths. We create truth by linking our conversations into a network of agreements. Human beings are communal creatures. We normally form communities, and we link our communities to each other by language as well as by trade. To survive as a species, our truth networks must mesh. Otherwise we'll just destroy each other.

Throughout the animal kingdom, *might* does seem to make *right*. We tend to believe the *winner* is always somehow *stronger*. We BELIEVE *might* wins. We BELIEVE that the strongest animal wins the battle and gains the herd. Human beings have lived by *belief* in *might*, in war and conquest, our entire history on this planet.

Can human beings live differently from animals?

I believe that *we, the people*, can live differently. We are animals, but we have more choices. Our ability to learn, retain, remember, and *know-how* has reached dazzling heights, as well as depths, recently.

Among the break-through possibilities is Reiki. It is a useful bandwidth, a bandwidth known for thousands of years by the practice of meditation to bring mental and emotional stability and clarity. The Reiki bandwidth functions harmoniously with other energies to bring beneficial results. The Reiki bandwidth admits us to a vision of unlimited potential for human life on this planet.

We are free and creative beings. I believe we can take the enormous step to figure out how to live together in peace. I believe we can figure out how to attain prosperity for all, without sacrificing our planet.

The Stars My Destination

This is the title of a book by Alfred Bester, published 1957 by Signet Books (ISBN-13: 978-1876963468). The content of the novel has escaped my memory, but the title still rings in me. The breadth of vision held by that title still impels me, so in the spirit of infinite expansion has this book been written.

Notice how social media has proliferated in such a short time. The social networks we naturally form are vital to us. We are aching to come together rather than living by individuality, boundaries and hostilities.

Truth is discovered by individuals but it must be upheld socially. I mean, the reason we go for *empirical* demonstration is that CONSENSUS is a major requirement by human beings for social reasons. We want to come to agreement, we want to SHARE our individual discoveries. We are social animals.

In other words, truth is attained by always moving toward agreeing with each other. We investigate with the intent to AGREE with each other on how to describe the universe and its functions. When the results of my experiment are the same as the results of you doing the same experiment, we have reached a – tentative – stage of truth. The more often our results match, the stronger our belief that we have discovered a new truth.

We create a planetary society. We want to communicate with each other, even when our natal languages are different. We can agree to disagree. Or, we can try to eliminate those people who disagree with us. If we stop moving toward basic agreements with each other, we create misunderstanding, war, and death.

The flip side of the Rensselaer study is, **it only takes 10% of us** with a willingness to hold our opinions about sustainability and peace FIRMLY. I invite you to join the peacefully expansive 10%, speak up, and also WALK our talk. I am happy and hopeful when I see the response from our sector since the election of 2016.

Reiki is a tool that works in harmony with the universe. When we use Reiki for ourselves, we clarify our minds, harmonize and balance our emotions, and gain strength to back up our well-considered opinions. When we ask Reiki to flow, we deliberately create a positive effect for whoever or whatever receives it.

Using the energy of Reiki, I believe we are riding the vibration of love. Divine Love. Divine Love is the Might that makes Right.

Love is a force that creates, heals and sustains. Reiki love heals and protects. Reiki love is safe. Reiki love is good for its giver as well as for its recipient.

Using Reiki without creating a contest between practices provides a path toward achieving a unified and peace-filled world.

I urge you to practice Reiki. Allow it to function in its time. Cultivate patience and hope as you learn to feel the effects of Reiki within you. Watch your progress into health and well-being. Allow the strength of its vibration to carry your thoughts into creativity and impel your attitudes toward positive actions. Choose Reiki as your way to participate in our planet's evolutionary shift in consciousness toward the peace and plenty we know we can have.

The End

Recommended Reading

Spontaneous Transformation Technique, Jennifer McLean, now (2018) out of print while a second edition is being prepared. Check out her website *www.McLeanmasterworks.com.*

A brief clear summary of Reiki-related science can be found in The Science Behind Reiki by Bernadette Doran, BS, RMT, *https://equilibrium-e3.com/reiki.php.*

Science Measures the Human Energy Field by J. Oschman in Reiki News Articles, The International Center for Reiki Training at *https://www.reiki.org/articles/science-measures-human-energy-field.*

Science and the Human Energy Field, an interview with James L. Oschman PhD, by William Lee Rand at *www.reiki.org.*

The Original Reiki Handbook of Dr. Mikao Usui, Mikao Usui and Christine M. Grimm, Lotus Press

1999 (ISBN: 9780914955573).

The Hayashi Reiki Manual, Frank Arjava Petter, Tadao Yamaguchi and Chujiro Hayashi, Lotus Press 2004 (ISBN: 9780914955757).

Hawayo Takata's Story, Helen J. Haberly, Archedigm Publications, Olney MD 20830, 1990 (ISBN: 9780944135068).

The Reiki Sourcebook, Bronwen and Frans Steine, O Books, Winchester U.K. 2003 (ISBN: 9781846941818).

Additional Resources

Sabine Hoehn
Author, editor, translator (English/German),
Reiki master/teacher, STT Practitioner, coach.
Email: *sabine.hoehn@t-online.de*
Skype: Sa Bine 898 (Sabine is a common name in
Germany.)

She has been my Development Editor and deserves
more credit than the Acknowledgements can
provide. Her understanding of emotional messages
being transmitted by subtle cues in language ranges
far beyond the expectation of someone who might
be viewed simply as a grammar and punctuation
editor, or German-English translator. Although she
welcomes routine work translating and editing,
she also shines as one whose command of English
could guide me into greater clarity as we explored
Reiki together.

Chellie and Mike Kammermeyer

ICRT Licensed Reiki Teachers, all levels, Holy Fire® II, Karuna Reiki ® and Reiki Drumming. See their website at: *www.InnerCompassReiki.com.*

Chellie and Mike are both teachers licensed by ICRT, and both are happy to work remotely as well as locally (Danville, CA). Mike's specialty is facilitating Reiki-enhanced Journeys by telephone; see their website for details.

Glossary

Reiki Terminology

Attunement – term given to a process by which the ability to emit Reiki is passed from Master to student.

Byosen – a compound noun in Japanese that refers to perceived disturbances in a person's energy field. Byosen are believed to indicate areas of the body that would relax if Reiki were applied.

Ignition – the word for Master's Attunement in the Holy Fire system.

Imbue – a verb used in Reiki practice meaning to direct Reiki toward an apparently inert object, intending to change the object by soaking it in Reiki.

Placement – the word for Attunement in the Holy Fire system of Reiki.

Reiki I, Reiki II, Reiki Master (some say Reiki III) – the three levels of Reiki established by Usui. (I suspect that people who do not feel comfortable in using the term "Master" when they are aware of other people who have special gifts are people who want the humility to say of themselves that they have attained the "Reiki III" level. I have heard the term "Grand Master" used to refer to a person with capabilities that may be unusual gifts. These are distinctions currently not under study).

In Japanese, the three levels of Reiki practice are:
Reiki I - Shoden ("first teachings"),
Reiki II - Okuden ("inner teachings"),
Reiki Master - Shinpiden ("mystery teachings").

Acronyms

CAM – Complementary and Alternative Medicine.

ECG/EKG – electrocardiogram.

EEG – electroencephalogram.

HCM – Hypertrophic Cardiomyopathy. The heart wall inside the left ventricle grows at an unpredictable rate and for no known reason.

MRI – magnetic resonance imaging.

NCCAM – National Center for Complementary and Alternative Medicine, formerly known as NCCIH (National Center for Complementary and Integrative Health).

NIH – National Institutes of Health.

PEMF devices – emit a Pulsing Electromagnetic Field. Since 1979 these have been approved by the

FDA to assist healing certain physical conditions.

PubMed® – a service of the National Library of Medicine. PubMed® contains publication information and in most cases brief summaries of articles from scientific and medical journals.

SQUID – superconducting quantum interference device – first measured very subtle bioenergies in the 60s.

Scientific Terms

bandwidth – a range of frequencies.

bioenergy – term widely used for renewable energy derived from recently produced biological sources. In this book, the term refers to energy produced by living cells.

blinding – The term *double blind* applies to a study set up so that no information is available to either the subjects or the control group that might affect their behavior.

coping (psychology) – a behavior pattern chosen to master, minimize or tolerate stress. The term *mechanism* is used to refer to coping behavior that has become automatic, instead of being behavior consciously chosen on the spot.

entrainment – "Any stable frequency evokes a cortical response. The brain synchronizes its dominant brainwave frequency with that of the external stimulus." (See Footnote 3 for source of this definition.)

epigenetics – the study of genes that express. Or not. Scientific excitement was generated by the discovery that the DNA string is not mechanistically controlling. Whether or not a gene is actively exercising its particular control is variable, depending on environmental conditions.

Healing Touch Program ™ – a therapeutic method similar to Therapeutic Touch.

Hertz – the term used to refer to the frequency of a vibration.

neuroplasticity – neural pathways are not fixed, so if a part of the brain is injured and usually-used pathways are damaged, the brain can create new neural pathways and rebuild some functions which were lost by the damage. This is sometimes referred to as *re-mapping*.

Therapeutic Touch – a practice of healing similar to Reiki. Practitioners believe that they are consciously directing or modulating an individual's energies by interacting with his or her energy field. It has a training and licensing system but does not employ attunements.

Cultural Term

Rishis (pl.) – In Hindu tradition, Rishis were seers or sages who lived in the Himalayas more than 5,000 years ago. They attained their wisdom by intense meditation, which led them to realize supreme truth and eternal knowledge. They passed on their understanding as hymns in the scripture known as the Vedas.

About The Author

Elizabeth Eddy, Ph.D., M.Div. and twice Reiki Master, was born a U.S. Army dependent, so the annual relocation exercised her natural flexibility and expectation that change is a normal part of life. At ten, her dad's deployment to Japan initiated several major themes in her life, among them writing and spiritual experience. She wrote her first book there and daily contemplated the peaceful vibration of a small Buddhist park she walked through daily.

Her Ph.D. in philosophy, 1970, focused on symbolic logic, but her dissertation expounded an aesthetic of form in music (which of course includes music as orderly vibrations – harmonic and rhythmic). Teaching as an adjunct at Florida Atlantic University ended with a call experience toward ministry as an Episcopal priest, a recently enabled field at the time.

Although her career included both ministry and secular employment, concurrently for 20 years, she discovered that her early attraction to spiritually as vibration could be satisfied by the practice of Reiki. Her first initiation in 1998 was followed by repeated trainings in 2005, and a Master's with William Lee Rand in 2007.

Ten years later, in 2016, retirement and open-heart surgery re-ignited her passion for Reiki, leading to a second Master's with William Lee Rand, in his Holy Fire® II system.

How Reiki Works draws together Elizabeth's aesthetic love of order and ethical desire to achieve harmony among all lovers of this planet. Her understanding of Reiki practice is founded on the expectation that these hopes and dreams can be achieved. Her goal is to provide Reiki to everyone who will practice it, for the physical, emotional and spiritual well-being of all beings.

Contact Elizabeth Eddy

Email:
e2@elizabeth-eddy.com

Websites
www.elizabeth-eddy.com

Address:
Geneva Enterprise LLC
446 Old County Road, Suite 100-234
Pacifica, CA 94044

Do you want to pursue Reiki further?

Now that you've seen the many ways Reiki could make a difference in your life, how do you take advantage? How to find a practitioner or teacher has been mentioned several times in this text. Along with learning and practicing Reiki for yourself, programs are available through the website *www.elizabeth-eddy.com.*

If you want Reiki-enhanced coaching from me, on problematic areas of your life, you are not required to have a Reiki attunement, although your experience will be much quicker if you do.

Career coaching and health coaching are my specialties.

Book a free Discovery call with me:

Together we discuss your hopes and needs, and reach an agreement on which package (see the following) is most appropriate for you. The call is also designed to check compatibility between coach Elizabeth and yourself as coachee.

Package possibilities:

Spot Treatment:

This is a three-month package of weekly coaching calls that focuses on a single particular area or aspect of your life. We'll nail down the area of your life you are ready to change, and proceed with vigor. We can stick to a single method, such as Jennifer McLean's Spontaneous Transformation Technique ("STT" for short), to release long-standing (perhaps even sub-conscious) conflicts. Or, we can add Law of Attraction methods to start a new growth pattern for you.

For "Me, Too" folk:

This book is aimed to introduce ordinary people to an extra-ordinary technique – Reiki. Among you may be persons who have suffered the particular trauma of sexual harassment. I have reasons not to write here about my personal experiences, but I DO have experience of the use of Reiki to heal myself of those memories. I know I can help you, too. CALL ME.

Get Organized for Your Future:

This is six-month package especially suitable for people who are already aware of strengths they want to build on. The aim is to create a personal system of growth toward goals, including new patterns of self-appreciation to spur achievement. Some STT release of old patterns may be involved.

The Time of Your Life packages are also available, usually 30 minutes each call, for four consecutive weeks. Each session offers Distant Reiki by me, in a three-part format: ten-minute (approximate) conversation about your needs, followed by a ten-minute break from the phone while you rest and receive a ten-minute burst of Reiki from me, and concluding with another brief conversation about your results, and how you can see yourself using your new attitude. This package may follow one or more episodes of the deep-diving Spot Treatment experience.

Acknowledgments

Thanks to the research librarians at one of the health libraries of the university teaching hospital where I serve on the Reiki Team. They spontaneously offered, and quickly provided, copies of relevant research material published in medical journals that gave me the push and encouragement to pursue answers where there seemed to be none.

Thanks to the wonderful woman who created our local Reiki Team, and sold the idea to two hospitals in our area. This is an outstanding accomplishment in spreading knowledge of Reiki in the community of people seeking medical treatment. Our team provides valuable experience of Reiki to patients, families and caregivers. I personally received from team experience the energy and vision that inspired "How Reiki Works." We in the team are grateful for this marvelous opportunity to serve.

Thanks to my Development Editor, Sabine Hoehn, whose questions and suggestions showed me where to expand my writing, and where I need exercise care to acknowledge variant opinions. Her many years of Reiki experience added aspects of Reiki practice that were new to me. Thanks to her for reading and commenting in detail on the manuscript, thanks for editorial skill, and thanks for contributing two of her own stories.

Lavish thanks also to another partner on this journey, Chellie Kammermeyer, for her major contributions to the Reiki story side of my text, and for her comments as a reader that kept me on track.

I can hardly recognize and thank enough my multitalented energy coach Elena, for her intense weekly work with me.

Thanks, too, to all contributors, named in the text and unnamed, for giving me such rich and beautiful material to share with all of you.

Thanksgiving for Pepper and Batcat, whose interruptions keep me grounded.

Many thanks and applause to A.R.E. (Edgar Cayce's Association for Research and Enlightenment, Headquarters in Virginia Beach, VA) and especially to Nancy Eubel, whose eGroups raised my vibrations during the four years that I took and retook every group she led.

Thanksgiving for the Get Your Book Done Program, by Christine Kloser. It was the trigger that ignited my dream to write, after 64 years of journaling, periodically dumping reams of notes, always wondering when my book would form. Get Your Book Done signaled to me that the time had finally come to write, and gave me the tools I needed to help shape the work.

Thanks for all the helpers along the way at Capucia Publishing, who created such a smooth and pleasant process.

Thanks to so many friends and close family, who believed in me and kept me going by their kind encouragement. I want to name you all.

Made in the USA
Monee, IL
16 August 2020

38567906R00138